Crime-Solving Science Projects

Forensic Science Experiments

Kenneth G. Rainis

Enslow Publishers, Inc.

40 Industrial Road   PO Box 38
Box 398   Aldershot
Berkeley Heights, NJ 07922   Hants GU12 6BP
USA   UK

http://www.enslow.com

For my sisters Patricia Griffiths and Kathleen Carney—
always caring, always supportive of big brother.
To Jack and Winnie Hosking—
two very special friends.

Library of Congress Cataloging-in-Publication Data

Rainis, Kenneth G.
    Crime-solving science projects : forensic science experiments /
Kenneth G. Rainis.
        p. cm. — (Science fair success series)
Includes bibliographical references and index.
Summary: Introduces various aspects of forensic science—document
examination, forgeries and counterfeiting, blood and DNA analysis, and
trace evidence and provides suggestions for related projects.
    ISBN 0-7660-1289-1 (alk. paper)
    1. Criminal investigation—Juvenile literature. 2. Forensic
sciences—Juvenile literature. [1. Forensic sciences. 2. Criminal
investigation.] I. Title. II. Science fair success.
    HV8073.8 .R35 2000
    363.25'078—dc21
                                99-050546

Printed in the United States of America

10 9 8 7 6 5 4 3 2 1

To Our Readers:
All Internet addresses in this book were active and appropriate when we went to press. Any comments or suggestions can be sent by e-mail to Comments@enslow.com or to the address on the back cover.

Illustration Credits: Courtesy Mr. and Mrs. Edd Carney, p. 82 (Mantle); Courtesy Neo/SCI Corporation, Rochester, NY, pp. 30, 32, 65, 98 (photos), 99, 100 (photos), 105, 110, 116; Michael Peres, RIT University (photos), pp. 22, 27; Kenneth G. Rainis (illustrations), pp. 15, 19, 22, 31, 33, 40, 51, 53, 59, 60, 64, 68, 70, 75, 80, 82 (Clinton), 89, 93, 98, 100, 104, 106, 114, 115, 121, 122.

Cover Photo: ©TSM/Bryan Allen

All quotes attributed to Sherlock Holmes were written by Sir Arthur Conan Doyle.

Acknowledgments

This book would not have become a reality without the loving support of my wife, Joan. Thanks to my partners at Neo/Sci: Kurt Gelke, George Nassis, and Jean Coniber, whose support is greatly appreciated. Special thanks to Ken Rando and Charissa Sullivan for their digital support. A special tribute goes to my daughter, Caroline, who tried, and almost succeeded, in copying her mother's handwriting used in these pages. To my sister Kathy and her husband Edd, whose "Mickey Mantle" autographs added a unique dimension to the book, and to Michael Peres of RIT University, who helped provide the spectacular photomicrographs.

Contents

Chapter 1

What Is Forensic Science, Anyway?

When you have eliminated the impossible, whatever remains, however improbable, must be the truth.

—Sherlock Holmes

With this book as your guide, you will explore how science is used to detect criminal acts. Forensic science is the body of tested knowledge obtained through the scientific method and used in a court of law to discover the truth. Each chapter of this book is designed around a particular aspect of forensic science—physical evidence, fingerprint analysis, document examination, forgeries and counterfeiting, blood evidence, and trace evidence. Within chapters, various methods of analysis are presented along with suggestions for exciting science fair projects. Each chapter will end with an unsolved case that will stretch your imagination. The clues to these cases lie within the book chapter. Additional technical information

and the answers to each chapter's unsolved casebook are in Appendix C.

The forensic scientist's skill is to use all the information available to find facts. For example, a forensic document examiner may be called on to state his or her expert opinion as to whether a document is genuine or has been altered.

Crime Laboratories

Forensic or crime laboratories vary greatly in the analyses and services they perform. The Federal Bureau of Investigation (FBI) Laboratory in Washington, D.C., is one of the largest and most wide-ranging forensic laboratories in the world. It can perform almost any analysis needed on physical evidence.

Other federal forensic laboratories serve specific federal agencies such as the Drug Enforcement Administration, or DEA (for illicit drug analysis), and the U.S. Secret Service (for counterfeiting). Many law enforcement agencies operate crime laboratories at the state, county, or local level. Some forensic laboratories are private organizations. Usually forensic laboratories are accredited—they have demonstrated a high level of quality control and accuracy.

Some careers in forensic science include the following:

- *Forensic laboratory technician*—a college-trained individual who collects physical evidence at a crime scene and processes or analyzes that evidence in the laboratory.

- *Forensic photographer*—a trained individual who records visual evidence at crime scenes and assists other forensic professionals in recording and analyzing various images of physical evidence.

TABLE 1-1. WHAT IS DONE IN A CRIME LAB?

Arson analysis	Detection of accelerants (substances that speed the spread of fire) in fire debris to prove arson
Firearms and toolmarks	Examination of firearms and ammunition, including scrapes or impressions on surfaces
Forensic photography/ videography	Documentation of a crime scene and physical evidence; comparison of trace evidence
Latent prints	Fingerprint, footprint, and shoeprint identification
Questioned documents	Comparison of inks, paper, and handwriting
Serology and DNA	Analysis and identification of body fluids and tissues
Toxicology	Isolation and identification of alcohol, drugs, poisons, and other toxic materials through use of forensic chemistry
Trace evidence	Dealing in small or trace quantities involving microscopic and/or microchemical analysis

- *Document examiner*—a trained individual who discovers and proves facts regarding documents.

- *Ballistics technician*—a trained individual who is an expert in the identification of firearms and recovered bullets.

- *Forensic psychiatrist*—a trained physician who is an expert in problems related to courtroom testimony dealing with behavioral and personality disorders, a person's understanding of facts to stand trial, insanity pleas, and psychological testing.

- *Forensic pathologist*—a trained physician who is an expert in finding the cause of wrongful death (not from accidental or natural causes).

- *Forensic anthropologist*—a trained scientist who is an expert in the identification of skeletal remains and, possibly, in determining cause of death.

- *Forensic odontologist*—a trained dentist expert in the identification of individuals through teeth and jaws, bite marks, and the analysis of facial trauma through abuse.

How Forensic Scientists Do Science

The procedure to learn the truth involves the following: observe, hypothesize, experiment and collect data, and draw conclusions.

As a beginning forensic scientist, you will work hard to observe what is happening. You will make a guess (a hypothesis) to explain what you observed. You will design a method (an experiment) to test your guess, and use your results (data) to conclude whether your guess was correct or whether it should be changed. Sometimes you will need to establish a control group against which to compare your results. A control helps a scientist link a planned change with an effect (or lack of effect) in the experimental group by comparison with the control.

Like the fictional detective Sherlock Holmes, your powers of observation of even the smallest detail will help you understand and eventually solve complex investigations. At times, your investigations will be aided by serendipity—the chance finding of something valuable while you are looking for something else. Although everyone has these experiences, they are meaningless unless you can know their value. As the great detective himself said: "There is nothing more deceptive than an obvious fact."

Recording, Analyzing, and Reporting Data

Data is unbiased information gathered through the scientific process. It can lead to knowledge and understanding. To be useful, data must be recorded, organized, and analyzed.

Reporting

Reporting your findings (conclusions) in a clear manner is critical to your success as a young scientist. Forensic scientists communicate their findings to law enforcement authorities and the courts through formal reports.

Your science fair project report should contain the following parts and be in this order:

I. Statement of problem. The question(s) that your project addresses.

II. Background. Information that relates to the question. Include a bibliography with at least three references.

III. Hypothesis. Statement of a possible answer to your question or a prediction of what you think might occur.

IV. Experimental design and procedure. A description of how you will test your hypothesis. Include all the steps that you will follow and include drawings or photographs to help in this explanation. List all the materials used to conduct your experiment(s). Make sure that you design a controlled experiment and can identify the planned change—variable or variables—in the experiment.

V. Results. A listing of all data (information) collected during the experiment(s). Use charts, graphs, photographs, or drawings to help organize data for easier understanding. When you make notes, be sure to include time, dates, and other observed experimental events.

VI. Conclusions. An understanding of your results as they relate to the hypothesis.

Check with your science teacher to see whether your science fair has a different format for reports. Either way, be very neat. The report should be typed or written clearly in blue or black ink.

Project Display

Check with your science teacher for your fair's rules on project displays. Presenting and displaying your project at school will usually require that you construct a display board.

Tools You Will Need

Most of the materials you will need as a junior forensic investigator can be obtained around the house or in local stores. Ask your science teacher for permission to use special instruments, such as a microscope or balance. Sources for other items are listed in Appendix A. Forensic techniques, including crime scene investigation and photography, close-up photography, using the microscope and making microscope slides can also be found in Appendix A.

Being Safe as a Junior Forensic Investigator

The most important ingredient for success is safety.

1. Be serious about science. An easygoing attitude can be dangerous to you and to others. Always experiment under the supervision of a knowledgeable adult.

2. Read instructions carefully and completely before beginning with any project in this book. Discuss your experimental procedure with a knowledgeable adult before you start. A flaw in your design could cause an accident. **If in doubt, check with a science teacher or other knowledgeable adult.**

3. Keep your work area clean and organized. Never eat or drink anything while conducting experiments.

4. Wear protective goggles when doing experiments involving chemicals or when performing any other experiment that could lead to eye injury.

5. Do not touch chemicals with your bare hands unless instructed to do so. Do not taste chemicals or chemical solutions. Do not inhale vapors or fumes from any chemical or chemical solution.

6. Clean up any spilled chemicals immediately. If you spill anything on your skin or clothing, rinse it off immediately with plenty of water. Then report what happened to a responsible adult.

7. Keep flammable liquids away from heat sources.

8. Always wash your hands with soap after conducting experiments with any microorganism. Dispose of contaminated waste or articles properly.

9. Be responsible when doing research on the Internet. Never give your name, address, or other personal information to anyone on the Internet without approval from your parent or guardian.

Chapter 2

Physical Evidence

It is a capital mistake to theorize before you have all the evidence. It biases the judgment.

—Sherlock Holmes

Every crime leaves visible signs called physical evidence. Physical evidence can be either in large or in trace amounts. It can show, after it has been scientifically examined and analyzed, that a crime has been committed. It can lead a careful investigator back to the perpetrator—the individual who committed the act. Some types of physical evidence—which include almost anything you can see—that are routinely examined by forensic scientists in crime laboratories include:

- Ballistics (firearms and projectiles)
- Body tissues and fluids, including blood
- Cosmetics
- Drugs and controlled substances

- Feathers
- Fingerprints, palmprints, and footprints
- Glass
- Gunshot residue
- Hair and fibers
- Marks and impressions
- Metal filings
- Paints
- Pollen
- Pyrotechnic and explosive materials
- Questioned documents
- Serial numbers
- Soils and minerals
- Woods and other vegetation

Marks and Impressions

Forensic investigators usually examine the following types of trace evidence—marks or impressions—at crime scenes:

- *Broken parts* having irregularly fractured edges
- *Impression marks* on smooth surfaces made by tires, fabrics, or fingers
- *Indented impressions* made on soft surfaces by feet or tires
- *Contact marks* or scratches left by hard edges scraping or shearing, such as tool marks

Investigation 2.1

Making Casts of Impressions

Materials

* sand or soil impression
* camera (optional)
* white card
* cardboard
* scissors
* stapler
* tablespoon
* plaster of paris
* container for mixing plaster of paris
* measuring cup
* water
* plastic bag
* soft brush
* ink pad (optional)
* rag (optional)
* graph paper (optional)

Select a distinct impression that you wish to cast, such as a footprint or tire mark in sand or soil. Photograph it, if possible, before casting. To improve the contrast in your photograph, use a white card to reflect light onto the impression from the side (see Figure 1a).

To create a 1-inch-high mold around the impression, cut some cardboard into 1-inch strips and staple them together to form one long strip. Bend and staple the cardboard strip into a circle or oval large enough to surround the impression. Position the cardboard mold in the soil or sand, surrounding the impression. The mold will aid in handling the cast (see Figure 1b).

Spoon 4 to 6 tablespoons of plaster of paris into a container along with approximately 1 cup of water. Use the tablespoon to mix the plaster of paris until it becomes thick. Stir it well but slowly to avoid creating bubbles in the plaster, which can produce holes in the cast.

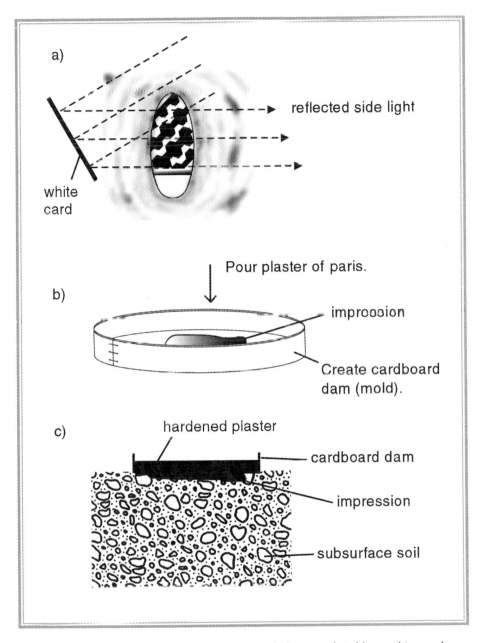

a) reflected side light

white card

Pour plaster of paris.

b) improooion

Create cardboard dam (mold).

c) hardened plaster

cardboard dam

impression

subsurface soil

Figure 1. a) Locate a suitable impression and photograph it. Use a white card to reflect light onto the sides of the impression, providing contrast around these edges. b) Create a mold and fill it with plaster of paris. c) Remove the mold and wipe it clean.

Carefully pour or spoon the mixed plaster into the mold. Fill to the top of the mold. Allow the plaster to harden overnight. It is a good idea to cover the mold with a plastic bag so that rain will not affect the plaster cast.

The next day, tap the top of the mold with your finger to confirm that the plaster has hardened. Carefully lift the mold and use a soft brush to gently remove any dirt or sand from the bottom of the cast. You may choose to remove the cardboard from the cast as well.

If the pattern on the bottom of the cast is difficult to see, you can use ink to give it more contrast. Apply some ink with a rag that has been dabbed on an ink pad. If you are making casts of a number of similar types of impressions (bicycle tire tracks, for example), you may want to use the inked cast as a stamp to make a print on a piece of graph paper. This will create a record sheet. The recorded markings can then be measured and compared.

Science Projects You Can Do

Information from a shoe impression

An individual who is walking, running, or jumping normally makes shoe impressions. Create a group of shoe impressions that can act as your impression database. Use this database to compare to unknown impressions. Your database should include prints that reflect these characteristics for both the right and left foot: slow gait (walk), fast gait, running gait, long jump from a standing position (of both the take-off and landing prints), various body weights, various shoe sizes, and various soil types and conditions: clay, mud, dry or soft soil, sand, etc.

Your investigation may point out that soil conditions can affect the appearance of an impression—for example, a shoe print in mud may look like it was made by a smaller shoe than it was. You may also observe that running creates an impression of a shoe that looks larger than it really is. Make a display that shows your method in obtaining impression data.

Estimate weight and height from a shoe impression.

From your experience in creating an impression database, develop a table that can accurately depict a person's weight and height using his or her shoe impression. For example, you may want to go to a shoe store and obtain measurement data that relates shoe size to inches. You may also wish to relate height to shoe size. Finally, you may want to weigh various individuals and measure the depth of their foot impressions in sand and in moist and dry soils. Although this information cannot provide a conclusive physical link to an individual, it is helpful in reconstructing a scene.

Present your findings in a display that highlights the relationship between shoe size, height, weight, and impression depth in various soils. In addition to your report, use charts and photographs to document your findings.

Estimate weight and height of a cyclist.

Use your analytical skills in reading shoe impressions to find out how the weight of a rider affects a bicycle impression. First, take an impression of a bicycle tire without a rider, then with riders of various weights. Most likely the differences in depth will be slight (unless the tire is underinflated), so you will need to analyze the amount of tire sidewall that is making the impression. Present your findings in a report and display that includes photographs that emphasize your experimental technique.

Investigation 2.2

Contact Traces: Becoming a Microprofiler

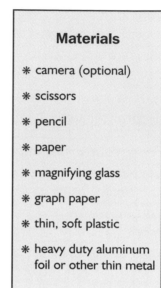
Tool edges can transfer their unique markings to the materials with which they come in contact. Examine individual tools to identify their edge microprofiles (i.e., unique marks). Use macro (close-up) photography (see Appendix A) to photograph a scissors' cutting edge. If this is not possible, make a pencil sketch of the tool's edge with the help of a magnifying glass. Make sure your sketch is accurate and to scale.

Use the scissors to cut a piece of thin, soft plastic or metal. Try to make the cut along as much of the blade length as possible. Either photograph or make a pencil sketch of the cut material's edge, looking for unique markings that correspond in spacing to that portion of the tool's cutting edge. Was there an identical transfer between cutting edge and impression material? Does an identical transfer need to occur? Use Figure 2 as a guide in creating an edge profile that is to scale.

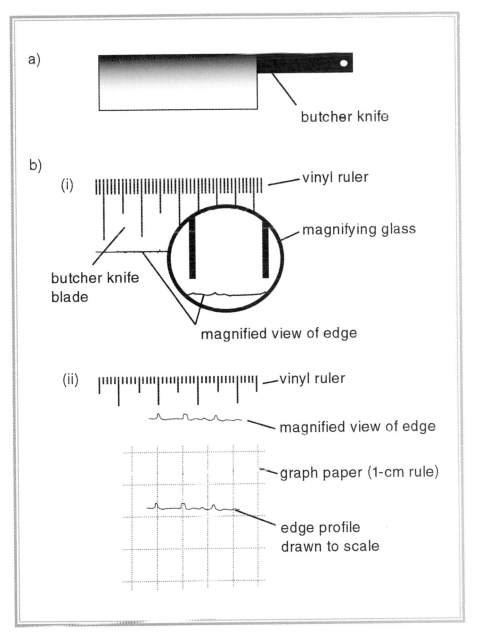

Figure 2. a) The cutting edge of a butcher knife can be used to create an edge profile. b) Drawing to scale: (i) Select and measure the area to be illustrated; position a scale (vinyl ruler). Observe edge using a 10X magnifying glass or stereomicroscope. (ii) Photograph the edge profile, including scale, or make a scale drawing using 1-cm graph paper.

A Science Project You Can Do

Find out the chance correspondence of two scratch marks.

Practice tightening and loosening a number of new nuts and bolts using the same socket wrench—without removing the wrench from the bolt. Use an adjustable or box wrench to hold the nut. Tighten at least 10 bolts in this fashion. Carefully examine the bolts and find out if a characteristic set of markings was placed on them by the socket wrench. Record and document all markings made on each of the bolts tested.

Find out the percentage of similar markings among bolts. Simply divide the number of similar observations by the total number of observations made. For example, if a similar marking was observed on three bolts out of a ten-bolt sample that was examined, the percent occurrence of the mark would be

$$\frac{3}{10} \times 100\%, \text{ or } 30\%.$$

Make additional tests using a different socket wrench for each group of five new bolts. Visit a local auto mechanic or hardware store and ask permission to test their wrenches. Again, calculate the percentage of similar markings among bolts.

Present your information in a table along with photographs and illustrations that support your conclusion concerning the identical appearance of chance marks. Are two different tools capable of creating the same mark on an object?

Investigation 2.3

Examining
Paint Chips

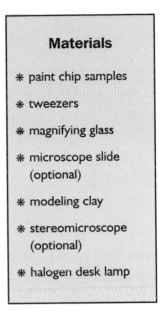

Materials

* paint chip samples

* tweezers

* magnifying glass

* microscope slide
  (optional)

* modeling clay

* stereomicroscope
  (optional)

* halogen desk lamp

A noted forensic scientist, H. J. Walls, once wrote, "One could almost claim for paint that it keeps the forensic scientist in business." His observation is most likely true when you consider that a very high percentage of crimes involve painted surfaces.

All paints have a solid portion known as the pigment. Pigment is responsible for the color of the paint. The liquid portion is called the vehicle or solvent. Paints are applied in liquid form and then converted to thin, hard film by either evaporation or oxidation. Paints that harden by evaporation of a solvent, such as car paints, become so hard that they break off in visible flakes. Paints that harden by the slower process of chemical change (oxidation), such as oil-based paints on buildings, tend to become detached as an elongated ribbon or smear.

One quick method of examining a paint chip is to simply pick up a flake or ribbon with tweezers and examine its edge using a magnifying glass. Be aware of which side is the inner or outer surface.

A more precise method is to mount the paint flake or smear on a microscope slide so that it is secure. Again, be aware of which side is the inner or outer surface. Mount the chip on a small piece of modeling clay so that its edge is at an upward angle (see Figure 3b). View the chip by using either a magnifying glass or a stereomicroscope at 40X. (A stereomicroscope magnifies fine details of objects visible to the eye.) Position a halogen desk lamp so that lighting is from above. Look carefully to observe the various layers of paint or primer.

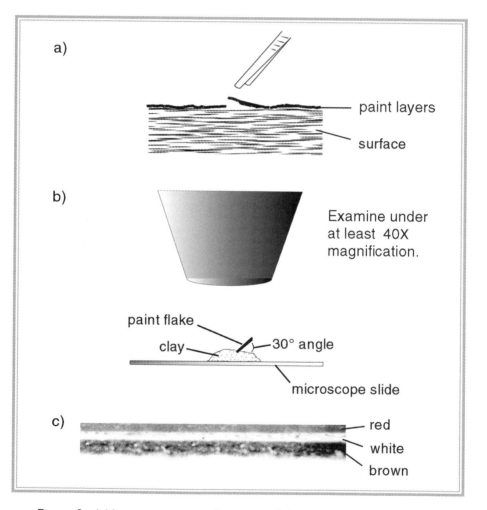

Figure 3. a) Use tweezers to collect paint flakes and smears. b) Examine the paint chip under a stereomicroscope. Record information through drawings or photographs. c) Magnified profile of an automobile paint chip (640X).

Science Projects You Can Do

What is in a paint job?

With an adult, visit an automobile junkyard. With permission from the owner, take paint flakes from various colored cars and examine them. Besides the outer finish coat color, observe the primer and undercoat color shades. Are they similar or identical? You can learn whether a particular car manufacturer uses a specific kind of primer and undercoat. Examine flakes using a magnifying glass (10X) or a stereomicroscope (40X), if possible. Make detailed colored-pencil drawings of your observations or record your findings using close-up photography (see Appendix A). Arrange your drawings and/or photographs of paint and underlying primer and undercoat colors by manufacturer and color. Do some manufacturers also use a clear overcoat? Use small envelopes to save paint chip samples for later comparison analysis. Have your friends present you with "unknowns" for you to identify.

Become a historic house paint analyst.

Obtain permission from the homeowner of an old home or outside structure to make an analysis of its paint. Visit the Welsh Color & Conservation Web site (www.welshcolor. com) to learn how house paint samples should be obtained. Try to find out the age of the home or structure. In your analysis, try to find out how many paintings the house has received over its lifespan. If possible, try to find out the average time between paintings. Also find out what colors were used. If possible, sample both trim and general exterior areas.

Investigation 2.4

Identification Based upon a Physical Property

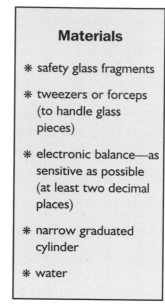

Materials

* safety glass fragments

* tweezers or forceps (to handle glass pieces)

* electronic balance—as sensitive as possible (at least two decimal places)

* narrow graduated cylinder

* water

Many common materials are difficult to describe. Although there are well over 100,000 kinds of glass, the vast majority (more than 99 percent) that is encountered in forensic investigations is ordinary soda-lime glass. Glass fragments from broken windows and car lamps can be given an identity only by determination of their physical properties. (The only way to conclusively match pieces of glass is through physically matching their edges.) Physical properties can provide valuable supportive information in a forensic investigation. One physical property that is universally used is density—the relationship between an object's mass and its volume. For glass, forensic scientists have calculated that the odds of finding two random pieces of glass matching in density is well over 800:1.

Use tweezers or forceps when handling glass fragments. Obtain half-inch-square (or larger) safety glass fragments from an automotive collision shop. Weigh a glass fragment on an electronic balance. The more sensitive your measurement, the more accurate your results. Measuring to at least two decimal places (0.01) is best.

To find the volume of the glass fragment, measure the amount of water it displaces. Accurately record the volume of water in a narrow graduated cylinder. Drop the fragment into the water and record the new volume measurement. Subtract the beginning volume measurement from the ending measurement. The difference is the volume of the glass fragment. (If you cannot see a large enough increase in the volume of water, weigh more than one piece and place them all in the cylinder.)

Divide the mass of the sample(s) by the volume of water it (they) displaced. For example, if a glass fragment weighs 7.40 grams and displaces 3 mL of water, its density would be:

$$\text{Density} = \frac{\text{Mass}}{\text{Volume}}, \text{ or } \frac{7.40 \text{ g}}{3 \text{ mL}} = 2.47 \text{ g/mL}$$

Science Projects You Can Do

Compare densities of various automotive glasses.

There are three types of glass commonly used on automobiles: safety glass in the windshield; tempered glass in the side and rear windows; and common soda-lime glass in headlights. In the library and on the Internet, research these three glass types to find out how they are made and why they are used. If possible, visit a couple of automotive glass sources (a junkyard or automotive window repair shop) and see if you can obtain pieces of each type of glass from each source. Take note of the visual appearance of any glass fragment. Safety glass breaks into square fragments, making its identification easy.

Find the densities of each of the glass pieces and compare them. For example, do glass windshield fragments from two different sources have identical densities? For window glass, your density calculations should range between 2.47 and 2.56 g/mL; for headlight glass the range would be 2.57 to 2.64 g/mL. Create a data table that lists use, glass type, mass, volume, and density. You might choose to make a poster that details how automotive glass is made and a report summarizing your density measurements.

Devise an experiment that demonstrates finding the density of a particular substance.

It does not matter what size sample you use. You do not need to use glass for the experiment. Try wood, plastic, or metal.

Determine whether all soda-lime glass is the same.

Suppose that as a forensic investigator, you are asked to determine if the soda-lime glass from a headlight manufactured outside the United States differs from that in one produced domestically. Construct an outline for your study and proceed to collect data such as the names of the domestic and international headlight manufacturers and the density of the glass for each lamp. Visit junkyards and auto glass repair shops to obtain samples. Generally, foreign-produced automobile parts have specialized markings. Use the Internet to obtain specific information from these manufacturers about their products. Write a science fair report; it should include your product search methods, density calculations, and close-up photographs (see Appendix A).

Casebook: Case of the Runaway Hot Rod

In a small town, a high school student was walking home one dark evening from his summer house-painting job when he was struck by a hit-and-run driver. Later that week, the local

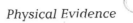

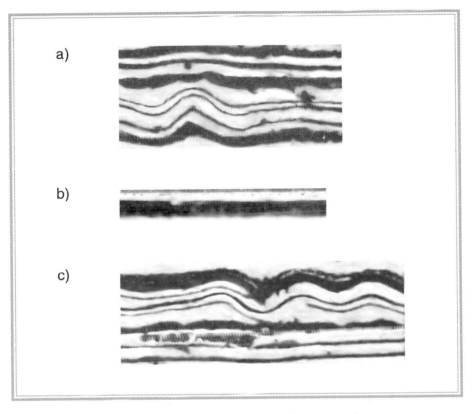

Figure 4. Evidence: "Paint Chip Comparison"

junkyard dealer received a request for a hood for a 1950s-style cruising machine. The alert dealer contacted authorities, who then determined that reasonable cause existed for a search of the youth's vehicle. This search revealed that there was a recent impact to the hood area of the vehicle. The authorities recovered paint chips from the hood of the youth's hot rod. These, along with paint fragments obtained from the clothing of the victim, are sent to you at the crime lab. You are presented with the three fragments shown in Figure 4: two recovered from the victim's clothing (4b and 4c) and one that was recovered from the suspect's vehicle (4a). Do any of these fragments match?

Chapter 3

Fingerprints

It was unquestionably the mark of his thumb.

—Sherlock Holmes

Fingerprinting, also known as dermatoglyphics, is an old science. It was known by the ancient Chinese, who recorded it in drawings on official wax seals attached to important state documents. Fingerprints and toe prints are caused by the presence of tiny ridges in the outer skin. They develop before birth. The arrangement and number of these friction ridges are unique to every individual. Although people had been aware of the fact that all individuals possess a unique combination of ridges on the hands and feet, the use of these print patterns for criminal identification was not accepted until the early 1900s.

The present system of fingerprint identification is based upon Sir Edward Henry's (1850–1931) first orderly classification scheme, which was modeled on the thumbprint. Henry established the first fingerprinting bureau with Scotland Yard in 1900.

In 1924, the Federal Bureau of Investigation (FBI) Identification Division was created. Over 750,000 fingerprint records, mostly from federal prisons, were transferred at that time to Washington, D.C. It was hoped that by having a single agency control information, criminal activity across state lines could be reduced. The FBI offers its identification services free of charge for official use to all law enforcement agencies in the United States.

Currently, the FBI possesses over 250 million sets of fingerprint records. This enormous collection is made up of both criminal and civil prints. Individuals who have been arrested are included in the criminal collection. The civil file includes the prints of government employees and applicants for federal jobs.

The FBI has developed a digital fingerprint analysis system that will completely replace the traditional fingerprint card. Known as the Integrated Automated Fingerprint Identification System (IAFIS), the new program will provide electronic national fingerprint checks. The new technology will allow police officers to take suspects' prints digitally, on a special electronic pad, and compare them almost immediately with millions of digitized prints on file in the FBI computer banks.

Increasingly, security access systems use fingerprints. In these systems, a laser is used to scan the ridge patterns of individuals who must press their fingers against a plate. This digital scan is then compared with stored data of security-cleared personnel. A match allows entry.

Fingerprint ridge patterns may be grouped into three large categories: the *arch*, the *loop*, and the *whorl*. In the arch pattern, the friction ridges extend across the bulb of the finger and rise slightly at the center. The loop pattern consists of one or more ridges curving into a hairpin turn. Ridges in the whorl pattern create a spiral or circle on the finger. These main groupings can be further divided into eight distinct patterns used for identification purposes, as shown in Table 3-1.

TABLE 3-1. FINGERPRINT PATTERNS

ARCH	LOOP	WHORL
Ridgelines start from one side of the fingertip, rise at the center, and exit on the other side of the fingertip.	Ridgelines start and end on the same side of the fingertip.	Ridgelines are circles that do not begin or end on either side of the fingertip.
Plain Arch	Radial Loop	Plain Whorl
Tented Arch	Ulnar Loop	Central Pocket Loop
		Double Loop
		Accidental Whorl

Making a Set of Fingerprints

To make a reference set of your fingerprints, label a white index card as shown in Figure 5. These types of prints are called direct prints by forensic investigators and are similar to those retained by the FBI. (All standard fingerprint cards are eight-inch-square pieces of coated card stock.)

Materials

✳ black inkpad or inkless fingerprinting cards (see Appendix B for sources)

✳ index cards—unlined (5 in x 7 in), white

✳ soap and water

✳ magnifying glass, 5–10X

RIGHT HAND				
1 Thumb	2 Index Finger	3 Middle Finger	4 Ring Finger	5 Little Finger

LEFT HAND				
1 Thumb	2 Index Finger	3 Middle Finger	4 Ring Finger	5 Little Finger

Left 4 Fingers Taken Simultaneously	Right 4 Fingers Taken Simultaneously

Figure 5. Fingerprint card design

To take a fingerprint impression, carefully roll each fingertip across the surface of the ink pad, then roll it in the center of the appropriate finger image area on the index card. Make sure that you obtain a clean set of impressions, otherwise repeat until you do. Wash your fingers with soap and water before retaking finger impressions or continuing with the investigation.

Use your magnifying glass to examine each fingerprint. Use Tables 3-1 and 3-2 to help you classify fingerprint patterns by category and by the location of various ridgeline details.

TABLE 3-2. IDENTIFYING FINGERPRINT RIDGELINE DETAIL

Ending ridge	▬▬▬	Hook	
Fork	⟨	Eye	⬯
Short ridge	▬	Double fork	
Dot	●	Delta	
Bridge	⟍	Triple fork	

Does each of your fingerprints have the same ridge pattern? Do they have the identical location of the same ridgeline detail? What differences are there in the ridge patterns of your left and right index finger and thumb prints?

Matching Fingerprints

When experts compare two fingerprints, they usually require 8 to12 points of similarity to establish that the prints are identical—that is, from the same individual. Use Figure 6 as a guide for obtaining an "identical match" of two fingerprints.

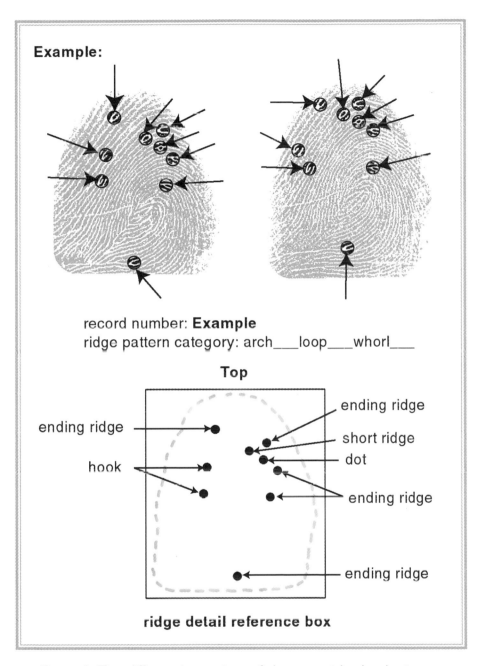

Figure 6. Two different impressions of the same right thumbprint are shown. Note that at least nine different matching ridgeline details exist, making these two prints "identical." The relative positions of each matching ridgeline detail are summarized in the reference box.

Science Projects You Can Do

Demonstrate an identical fingerprint match.

Make two separate right thumb impressions from the same finger, each on a white index card. Use a magnifying glass to study both fingerprints. Circle 8 to 12 positions where the same ridgeline detail occurs in both thumbprints. Use Figure 6 as a guide. Are these two fingerprints identical, or did you just prove an identical match?

Which pattern category is most uncommon?

Make and study at least 100 impressions (from 10 or more individuals). Use a magnifying glass to study and classify each print. Record your results in your notebook by creating a table that lists each numbered fingerprint impression and the corresponding category type—arch, loop, or whorl. Sort your findings and create a chart of your results showing the percentage of each category type. Does gender (male or female) influence category type? Are any other variables (for example, race or hair color) related to your findings?

Do identical twins have unique fingerprint patterns?

Take fingerprint impressions from as many sets of identical twins as you can. Examine and compare each finger in order. What do you conclude? Prepare a poster that illustrates one example. Use a copier to enlarge a single fingerprint (from the same finger) from each twin. Lay these enlarged prints side by side and identify areas of similarity and dissimilarity. If the twins' prints are not the same, are they more similar to each other than non-twin siblings? Two unrelated people?

Investigation 3.2

Studying Latent Fingerprints

Materials

* some friends
* black inkpad or inkless fingerprinting cards (see Appendix B for sources)
* index cards—unlined (5 in x 7 in), white
* dry cloth
* microscope slides
* drinking glass
* graphite powder (from art supply store)
* newspaper
* dust mask
* disposable polyethylene gloves
* 2 oz paper cups
* makeup brushes with very soft bristles
* camera (optional)
* clear tape
* scissors
* magnifying glass, 5–10X
* talcum powder
* paper, wood, metal, cloth surfaces

Latent, or hidden, prints are impressions caused by perspiration on the ridges of the skin. Perspiration contains water, salt, amino acids (the building blocks of proteins), and perhaps oil, dirt, grease, or blood. The method used for obtaining latent prints depends upon the type of surface the prints were left on, the manner in which the prints were left, and the quantity of material left behind.

You can try this activity with a couple of your friends. Take a reference set of direct prints from each individual, as you did with your own in Investigation 3.1.

Using a dry cloth, wipe a glass microscope slide (or other glass object, such as a drinking glass) free of any fingerprints. Handle the microscope slide only by the edges. Close your eyes and have one of your friends (without telling you who) rub his right thumb against his nose or forehead (to collect skin oils) and place his right thumbprint in the center of the microscope slide.

Use graphite powder as your dusting powder. **Graphite is very slippery! Protect working surfaces with newspaper to collect any excess graphite. Do not inhale any graphite dust! Wear a dust mask and disposable gloves whenever you work with graphite powder.** Place a *small* amount of graphite powder in a small paper cup, just enough to cover the bottom. Dip a soft makeup brush into the cup and lightly dust the suspected area containing the print. After the print is imaged, remove excess graphite powder by gently brushing it away. Be careful not to destroy the print with too hard a brush stroke! This technique requires practice. (Try it out on your own fingerprints first before you try to lift an unknown fingerprint.)

If you have a camera available, try to photograph the developed print. Appendix A contains directions for photographing forensic evidence.

To lift the print from the glass to an index card, unroll about 5 or 6 inches of clear tape and place the end to the right of the developed print, keeping some of the left end free so that you can remove the tape. Allow the rest of the tape to cover the print. Carefully smooth the tape over the developed print to force out all air bubbles.

Remove the print by pulling up on the free end of the tape and place it (print side down) on a clean white index card. Cut off the edges of the tape.

Observe the print with a magnifying glass. Compare this print to your reference file of fingerprints. Can you get an identical match?

When dusting for fingerprints on dark surfaces, use white talcum powder instead of graphite powder. Also, use a different brush for each type of dusting powder.

Have your friends handle or touch a variety of objects or surfaces, such as paper, wood, metal, or cloth. Use your newly acquired skills as a forensic investigator to lift and identify latent fingerprints. Recently, the FBI was successful in catching a poisoner by tracing his fingerprints to certain library books.

Science Projects You Can Do

Evaluate surfaces for ease of lifting latent (hidden) fingerprints.

Make a collection of samples of various common surfaces. Some examples might include glass, paper, wood, plastics, linoleum, metal, cloth, painted surfaces, and wallpaper. Wipe the test area of each of these surfaces clean using a handkerchief. Make fingerprint impressions using the same fingers on each surface. Use the latent print technique to lift the fingerprints from each surface type. Can an entire print or only a partial print be lifted from each surface? Devise a method to rank each surface in terms of print recoverability. Create a poster that illustrates your findings.

Determine how latent fingerprints are made.

Perspiration is known to play a central role in creating latent fingerprints. Test this factor by making latent fingerprints on a clean, smooth surface, free of any previous fingerprints, with (a) hands that have been just washed and carefully dried, (b) hands that have not been washed for a while,

(c) newly washed hands treated with a skin moisturizer, and (d) sweaty hands after vigorous exercise. Try lifting prints from each of these four classes of hands. Do these trials at least ten times. Use the same latent-print-lifting technique to lift the prints from each test surface. Record your findings in your notebook. Can you readily lift a certain class of latent fingerprints? Do your results support this finding? Do oils (such as in skin moisturizers) have any effect? On a poster, illustrate your findings with xerographic enlargements of various lifted prints.

Determine whether latent fingerprints improve with age.

Wipe off a clean, smooth surface so that it will be free of any fingerprints, and make a series of "good" latent fingerprints on it. Make a mark to identify the surface having the latent fingerprint. Place half of these surfaces with fingerprints on a windowsill that receives direct sunlight, and half in a closet. Leave them for several days. Use the same latent-print-lifting technique to lift the prints from each test surface. Is there any difference in your ability to lift latent prints from an exposed or nonexposed surface? Try longer time periods, such as 1 week, 2 weeks, 1 month, or as long as you can. Based upon your investigations, do latent fingerprints improve with age? Does exposure to sunlight improve or fade the prints over time? On a poster, illustrate your findings with xerographic enlargements of various lifted prints.

Investigation 3.3

Identifying Direct Prints

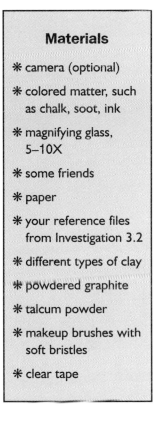

Materials

* camera (optional)
* colored matter, such as chalk, soot, ink
* magnifying glass, 5–10X
* some friends
* paper
* your reference files from Investigation 3.2
* different types of clay
* powdered graphite
* talcum powder
* makeup brushes with soft bristles
* clear tape

Sometimes criminals will leave behind prints that are clearly visible. These will have been made by colored matter on the fingers: blood, soot, ink, dyes, etc.

Have one of your friends from Investigation 3.2 make some direct prints on pieces of paper (without telling you who did it). Compare this print to those in your reference files. (If possible, photograph the direct prints in the "field" and have enlargements made for later examination and comparison.) Can you make a positive identification? Can you definitely rule out other individuals? Remember, print examiners usually require 8 to 12 points of similarity between two prints to establish that the prints were from the same individual.

Try making direct plastic prints in clay, Silly Putty, and similar materials. How effective are these materials in recording clear fingerprints? Using the techniques described in Investigation 3.2, can you dust and lift fingerprints from these materials?

Casebook: Case of the Digital Image

Sean Kaprikosh thought he had an opportunity to make a lot of money. As head of the city's crime lab, he was in charge of the fingerprint division. A police officer for twenty-five years, he thought he knew all the ropes. Since the FBI now required that all fingerprint files be sent in a digital format, he saw his chance.

Captain Kaprikosh planned to digitally alter fingerprints, for the right price, of people who wanted to escape forensic detection. He assumed that if he sent a digital set of finger-prints to the FBI, the old fingerprint file would be updated and replaced.

You are an FBI fingerprint examiner. There is a question about an individual's fingerprint file due to a mismatch between an old file and a new digital file that bears an iden-tical name and social security number. A right thumbprint from each file is presented to you (see Figure 7). What do you do? Write a report that summarizes your analysis.

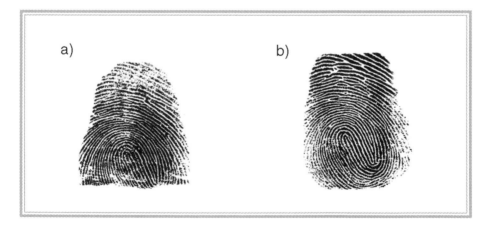

a)   b)

Figure 7. Fingerprint (a) is currently on file with the FBI. An updated digital printout of (b) is also presented. There is a question as to whether both these prints are from the same individual. Print (b) appears to be altered. Acting in your role as an expert fingerprint examiner, analyze both prints.

Chapter 4

Examining Documents

It would be a poor expert who could not give the date of a document within a decade or so.

—Sherlock Holmes

A document is the product of a combination of several materials. Pigment and paper are put together by means of an instrument such as a pen, pencil, typewriter, or electronic printer. When a document is suspected of being fraudulent (a misrepresentation), it is called a questioned document. The document examiner discovers and proves facts regarding documents. The bulk of the examiner's caseload rests upon answering questions regarding authorship, authenticity, alterations, additions, and erasures. However, a document examiner may be asked to find out the significance of inks, paper, writing instruments, business machines, and other tools used in preparing documents. Following examination, a report is filed regarding examination findings. The examiner stands ready to present these findings as an expert witness. This chapter will show you how a document examiner conducts investigations of questioned documents.

There are two quite distinct areas within document analysis. One involves the examination of the visual characteristics of handwriting in order to establish the identity of the writer. The other involves establishing what instruments and materials were used to prepare documents.

Writing Implements and Machines

There are many kinds of handheld instruments, as well as other mechanical and electronic devices, used to apply ink or graphite to create a document. With care and practice, you can learn to identify each type.

Types of Writing Implements

Pen: An instrument that applies liquid ink to a surface.

Quill: 6th century A.D.
Quill and nib pens produce a double-track line stroke having darker margins with uniform distribution of ink.

Steel Nib (dip style): 1830s
User needs to recharge ink supply; quill and steel nib pens thus produce variable ink densities.

Steel Nib (fountain): 1884
Ink density remains constant; no recharging.

Ballpoint: 1945
Uniform distribution of ink across width of line; usually leaves center indentation markings.

Roller: 1960s

Uniform distribution of ink across width of line; no indentation marks; line has quality of fountain pen.

Fiber-tip: 1964

Uniform distribution of ink across width of line; width of line varies with size of tip.

Pencil: An instrument containing a core of solid marking substance within a holder.

Graphite: 16th century

Particles of solid graphite cling to paper fibers. The amount of graphite mixed with clay following baking determines hardness.

Mechanical: A machine that can reproduce printed characters on paper.

Typewriter, adding machines, calculators, and cash registers: 1870s (lever strike), 1961 (ball and strike electronic typewriters)

Each manufacturer designed similar typefaces individually. Ink supplied through a movable ribbon.

Electronic: A computer output device that records information on paper.

Impact Printer: 1950s

Type arranged on a metal type ball or plastic disk (daisy wheel). Ink supplied through a ribbon.

Dot Matrix: 1960s

Characters formed as a pattern of dots. Ink supplied through a ribbon.

Ink-jet and laser printers: 1980s

Solid toner electrostatically applied to paper via electronic template. Smudging observed around individual characters.

Investigation 4.1

Are Dot Matrix Patterns Unique?

Materials

❊ printing samples from dot matrix printers

❊ scissors

❊ white glue

❊ index card, white

❊ photocopier that enlarges

❊ magnifying glass, 5–10X

Find out if dot matrix character patterns are unique enough to identify an individual printer manufacturer. Obtain printing output samples (of the same font and type size) from as many different dot matrix printer manufacturers as possible. From each manufacturer, select 10 characters (letters, numbers, symbols; upper- and lowercase) for a detailed comparison. Use scissors to cut out each character and paste it on the left-hand side of a clean white index card. Label the back of each card with the manufacturer's name, font, and type size. Use a photocopier to equally enlarge each character so that dot inspection will be easier—even though you will be using a magnifying glass. Cut out each enlargement and paste them on the right-side area of the index card. Compare like characters (and sizes) from each manufacturer. Can you find a difference among manufacturers and thus be able to associate a particular typescript to a certain printer manufacturer? Create a poster that illustrates your analysis methods, results, and conclusions.

Investigation 4.2

What Type of Colorant Is Used in India Ink?

Inks are fluids and pastes used for writing and printing. The oldest preserved writings were made with inks based on carbon black, a finely ground pigment in water or oil. Other ancient inks were made from indigo (a blue dye from plants); from the galls (swellings caused by insects) of oak and nut trees; from tannin (another plant substance); and from the inky fluids secreted by octopus and squid.

Most inks are made of a colorant and a liquid or paste vehicle. The colorant provides the ink's color. Colorants are made from dyes, which dissolve completely in the liquid or paste, or from pigments, which remain suspended in it. The vehicle helps bind the colorant to the paper. Vehicles have no color. The most popular liquid vehicles are water, alcohol, petroleum, mineral oil, and vegetable oil. Most writing inks dry when the liquid vehicle has evaporated and the paper has absorbed the colorant. Forgers use hypochlorite—laundry bleach—to remove dye-based inks; pigment-based inks cannot be removed by bleaching.

Place a drop of distilled water in the center of a clean microscope slide. Add a small drop of India ink. Mix with a toothpick. Add a coverslip and observe the slide under high-dry magnification (430X) of a compound microscope. (A compound microscope provides a high magnification view of microscopic objects; a stereomicroscope provides a magnified view of standard-sized objects.) The presence of millions of tiny dots (particles) indicates a pigment; a lack of particles indicates a dye. Try this examination technique with other water-soluble writing inks, such as colored calligraphy inks.

You can see how ink resins work by obtaining a ballpoint pen having erasable ink. Unlike most writing inks, this ink type is not readily absorbed by paper. Instead, the resin at first binds the pigment only to the surface of the paper. The resin and pigment can then be erased without damaging the paper—but only for a short time. The paper absorbs the ink over time. Experiment to find out just how long.

Types of Writing Inks

Carbon Black
An ancient ink that is still employed today in certain water-based drawing inks (such as India ink).

Iron-gall
A water-based solution of an iron salt and a tannin; developed during the Middle Ages. Low pH (acidic) ink. As this ink ages, its color turns from black to rust (brown). Ultimately improved 100 years ago to become the modern blue-black ink with the addition of a blue dyestuff.

Quick-drying: 1930s
Water-soluble fountain pen inks. Their high alkalinity (pH 11–12) makes them soak quickly into paper, eliminating blotting.

Paste: 1940s

Ballpoint inks are thick and pastelike, using organic chemical solvents instead of water. Similar type is used in typewriter ribbons.

Contemporary: 1970s

Fluid water-based inks used in porous or fiber-tip pens and roller ball pens.

Gel: 1990s

Although water-based, these pigment inks contain additional solvents that evaporate rapidly and make the ink waterproof. They are fade- and bleach-resistant. Some inks have fluorescent pigments.

Invisible Inks

Invisible inks have been in use since around A.D. 600. They have routinely protected important communication. George Washington and his officers regularly used invisible inks—which they called stains—to convey important military information concerning British troop and ship movements during the British occupation of New York (1776–1781). His intelligence officers applied a "counterpart liquid" to the document to read messages.

Invisible inks are generally of two types: sympathetic and organic. Sympathetic inks, visible when applied, turn colorless as they dry. When other chemicals, called reagents, are later applied, the colorless writing becomes visible. Organic inks are natural substances such as vinegar, milk, and fruit juices, which are made visible by the application of heat.

Investigation 4.3

How Invisible Inks Work

Materials

* an adult
* red cabbage
* measuring cup
* pot of water
* stove
* timer
* 2 paper cups
* lemon juice or vinegar
* toothpicks
* several sheets of thin white paper
* magnifying glass, 5–10X
* lamp with a 100-watt lightbulb
* notebook
* cotton swabs
* pH paper (optional)
* eyedropper (optional)

Shred about 1 cup of red cabbage and, **under adult supervision**, boil it for 20 minutes. The water will turn red. The color is from natural anthocyanin pigments. Allow the solution to cool.

Place a small amount of cooled cabbage water into a paper cup. Fill another paper cup with lemon juice or white vinegar.

Dip a toothpick into the colorless vinegar or lemon juice and use it to write a message on each of two sheets of thin white paper. Allow time for the messages to dry completely. Examine the sheets with a magnifying glass.

Take one of the paper sheets and hold it near a glowing 100-watt lightbulb. **CAUTION: A 100-watt bulb is very hot! Be careful when holding the paper near it.** Record what happens in your notebook. Be sure to examine the sheet again with a magnifying glass. Since these organic inks are made visible through the application of heat, only one of the sheets will show signs of writing.

Using cotton swabs, apply colored cabbage water over the area of writing on the other sheet of paper. Record what happens in your notebook. Be sure to examine the sheet again with a magnifying glass.

Hints to aid your investigation

- Use pH paper to check the cabbage water and vinegar or lemon juice. Record your results in your notebook. Which solutions are acidic? Which are basic? Acids have a pH range from 6 to 1—the lower the number, the more acidic. Bases have a higher pH range: from 8 to 14. Substances with a pH of 7 are neutral.

- Try mixing equal volumes of cabbage water and lemon juice or vinegar in a cup. Again measure the pH. Record your observations in your notebook. Does this reaction help explain how a sympathetic ink works?

- Use an eyedropper to place single drops of vinegar or lemon juice, spaced apart, on another sheet of thin paper. Use your magnifying glass to see how an acid affects paper. Do bases affect paper in the same manner?

Write a report in which your hypotheses and conclusions are stated and supported. Based upon your experimental data, can you improve these invisible inks?

Investigation 4.4

Ink Molecules Up Close

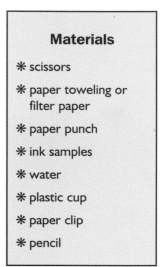

Materials

* scissors

* paper toweling or filter paper

* paper punch

* ink samples

* water

* plastic cup

* paper clip

* pencil

Since the late 1950s, chromatography has been used to compare and identify inks. Chromatography ("color writing") separates and identifies components of mixtures. You can use this exciting technique to investigate the nature of various ink dyes.

Cut out a strip of paper toweling 6 in x ¾ in (15 cm x 2 cm). Cut a point on one end of the strip. Using a paper punch, punch a hole through the other end (see Figure 8a).

Place a small spot of blue fountain pen ink or ink from a fiber-tip pen near the point of the paper and allow it to dry. Repeat this step about four times to build up the ink spot.

Put about 1 inch (2 to 3 cm) of water in a plastic cup. Open a paper clip. Place it through the hole in the paper so that you can hang it from a pencil (see Figure 8b). Position the paper strip so that it hangs in the center of the cup without touching the sides. Only the tip of the spotted end of the paper toweling should be touching the water. Do not submerge the ink spot in the water.

The water will rise on the paper toweling through capillary action (the rising of a liquid when in contact with a solid). When it reaches the ink spot, it will continue rising with or without some of the ink. (If the ink dyes are soluble in water,

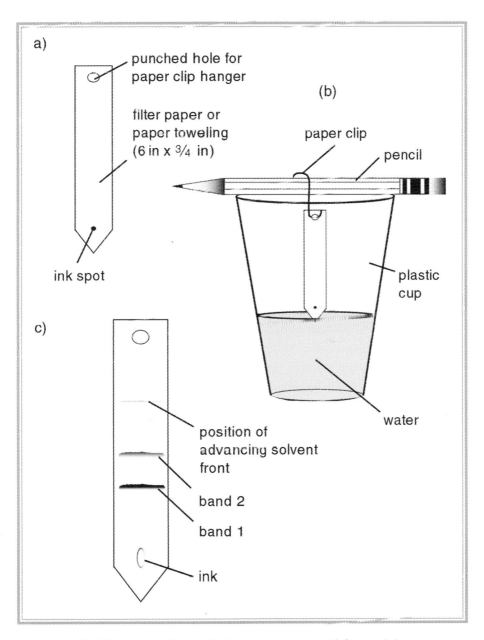

a)

punched hole for
paper clip hanger

(b)

filter paper or
paper toweling
(6 in x ¾ in)

paper clip

pencil

ink spot

plastic
cup

c)

position of
advancing solvent
front

band 2

band 1

water

ink

Figure 8. a) Place a small spot of ink on a paper strip. b) Suspend the paper strip so that its point just touches the solvent (water). c) Completed chromatogram.

the water will carry dye molecules with it as it travels up the paper. If the ink dyes are not soluble, the water will not carry dye molecules with it.) Notice how the dye colors that make up the ink separate as the water "solvent front" moves up the paper towel. The lighter pigment molecules travel farthest up on the paper towel; heavier pigment molecules (or solid pigments) do not travel as far. The resulting image is called a chromatogram. A chromatogram is like a fingerprint, a visual way to show all the individual dye colorants present in an ink sample, separated by their molecular size.

Science Projects You Can Do

Compare various inks using chromatography.

See how many different dye colorants are used to make the various writing inks in fountain pen, fiber-tip, and roller ball inks. Do certain colored inks from different pens have identical chromatograms? Which pens use inks with the most dye mixtures? Create a poster that both illustrates how to make a chromatogram and shows some selected chromatographic data that support your hypothesis.

Forensically analyze writing samples to detect an altered document.

Using chromatography, see whether certain writing samples contain identical inks. Have a friend submit a writing sample in which two inks (of different manufacturer but of the same color) are used. The sample should be written with mostly one ink. The second ink should be used in a small section of the sample. By looking at the writing sample, you should see no difference in inks. But you can find out what

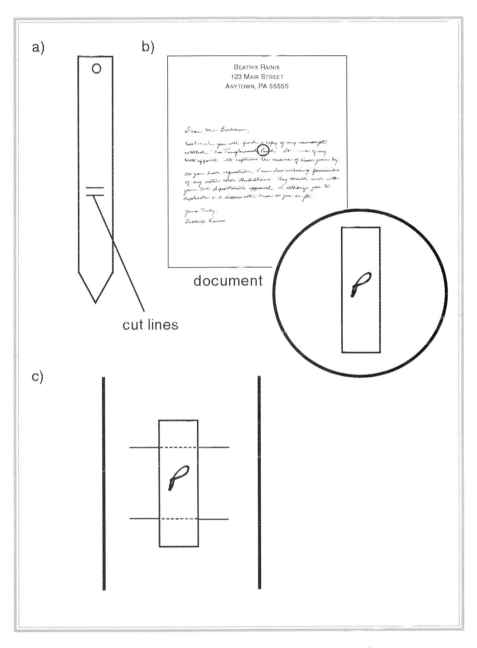

a)

b)

BEATRIX RAINIS
123 MAIN STREET
ANYTOWN, PA 55555

document

cut lines

c)

Figure 9. a) Use a razor knife to cut two slits in a prepared paper strip.
b) Cut a letter from a document. c) Position the cut letter in between the
two slits cut in the paper strip. Run the chromatogram.

part of the document was altered with different ink by analyzing the inks. Using a razor knife, cut two slits in a chromatography paper strip, as illustrated in Figure 9a. Then use the knife to cut out a strip from the document that contains individual character(s) with a good amount of ink—such as *g* or *h* (see Figure 9b). Carefully insert the cutout strip from the document through the two slits cut on the filter paper. Repeat this procedure with another chromatography strip and a new strip of paper that holds a letter within a suspect writing sample. Make sure both samples are placed at approximately the same distance from the tip of the paper so that the chromatograms will be consistent (the dyes will travel over the same distance). Run both chromatograph tests as explained in Investigation 4.4. Compare the results with that of the known chromatograms you made of commercial inks in the previous science project.

Run additional chromatograms from writing samples taken from various parts of the document. Can you conclude which portion is the "original" and which areas are additions? Create a report that details your scientific analysis, results, and "expert" opinion. Have your friend (the "forger") confirm the accuracy of your conclusions.

Investigation 4.5

Studying Document Alterations

When suspicion of fraud exists, document examiners try to reveal evidence of the fraud.

Ask your classmates to provide documents for you to analyze. Examples could include past homework assignments, classroom notes, written notes from a notepad, and photocopies. Try to review at least fifty documents, looking for signs of alteration: erasures, obliterations, and indented writing. Use the standard detection procedures outlined in Table 4-1 as you work. Compile counts of alterations by type and by document, summarizing them in a table. Create a poster chart that lists the frequency and type of each document alteration. Include examples for each type of alteration.

A Closer Look at Handwritten Documents

Handwriting is unusual because the trace of the crime—the ink line—is also the crime itself.

The identification of handwriting is based on the supposition, "People are all alike; people are all different." To be able to make a positive identification of a person's handwriting, a document examiner must be able to see the distinguishing individual writing characteristics that separate one person from all others. If two writings by the same individual are compared, there will be similarities without any major dissimilarity.

TABLE 4-1. DOCUMENT ALTERATION

Type	Technique	Method of Detection
Erasures	Chemical: Use of a bleaching agent	UV light reveals staining.
	Abrasive: Use of an eraser or sharp instrument	Magnifying glass reveals disturbance of paper fibers.
Obliteration	Use of correction fluid	Direct light reveals opaque area; hold object in front of lamp.
Indented writing	Writing on paper that is on top of other sheets of paper; indentations may appear on bottom pages depending on pen pressure.	Rubbing of soft lead pencil across sheet bearing indentations; using side- (oblique-) angle lighting techniques.
Photocopying	Optical or physical manipulation by overcopying or recopying	Careful examination of the document. • Use letter-spacing analysis. • Check for magnification alteration, background flaws, type incompatibility, or stray markings.

Handwriting Examination

Disguised handwriting (cursive script)

An attempt to remove or modify an individual's normal writing habits. Usually all that is achieved is a change in the pictorial appearance of the writing, while the distinguishing characteristics are rarely affected.

Hand printing

A disconnected style of writing in which each letter is written separately and includes block capitals. Often found in anonymous letters as a means of hiding the identity of the writer. This writing style is one of the most frequent disguises used by the anonymous letter writer and is quite effective if no specimen of hand printing is available for comparison.

The method of identifying hand printing is the same one used for cursive script—the improbability of a number of individual characteristics accidentally coinciding in two writings from different sources.

Numerals

Each writer is identifiable by his numerals in the same general manner as outlined above.

To make a valid comparison, the document examiner needs adequate samples. These should be of the same kind as the questioned writing. An examiner can normally compare only capitals with capitals, *A*s with *A*s. Capitals cannot be compared with lowercase writing, or *A*s with *B*s. The samples should be as close to the same age as the questioned document as possible. There should be at least five samples to show the normal range of the individual's handwriting.

Investigation 4.6

Comparing Writing Samples

Materials

* photocopier
* notebook
* writing samples
  (5 authentic, 1 forged)
* razor knife
* white glue

Comparing writing samples, one in question against five authentic samples, involves close examination of each letter. Look for significant matches or mismatches, first in form (general pen movements) of the letter, and also in the fine detail of each letter formation. Use Figure 10 as an example.

Use the following as a checklist for your comparison:

- significant matches or mismatches in the form of the letter

- fine detail of letter formation

- relative proportions and sizes of letters

- parts of compound letters, such as *k* and *g*

- parts of letters that may be conventional or unusual in style; flourishes and ornamentations

- slant, from backhand to forehand slope

- links or spaces between each letter

- relative height of each letter above the line

- quality of the pen line itself: whether it is smooth, tremulous, jagged, confident, or contains pauses and odd pen-lifts.

Without your knowledge, have a friend produce for your examination a set of six documents in which either all

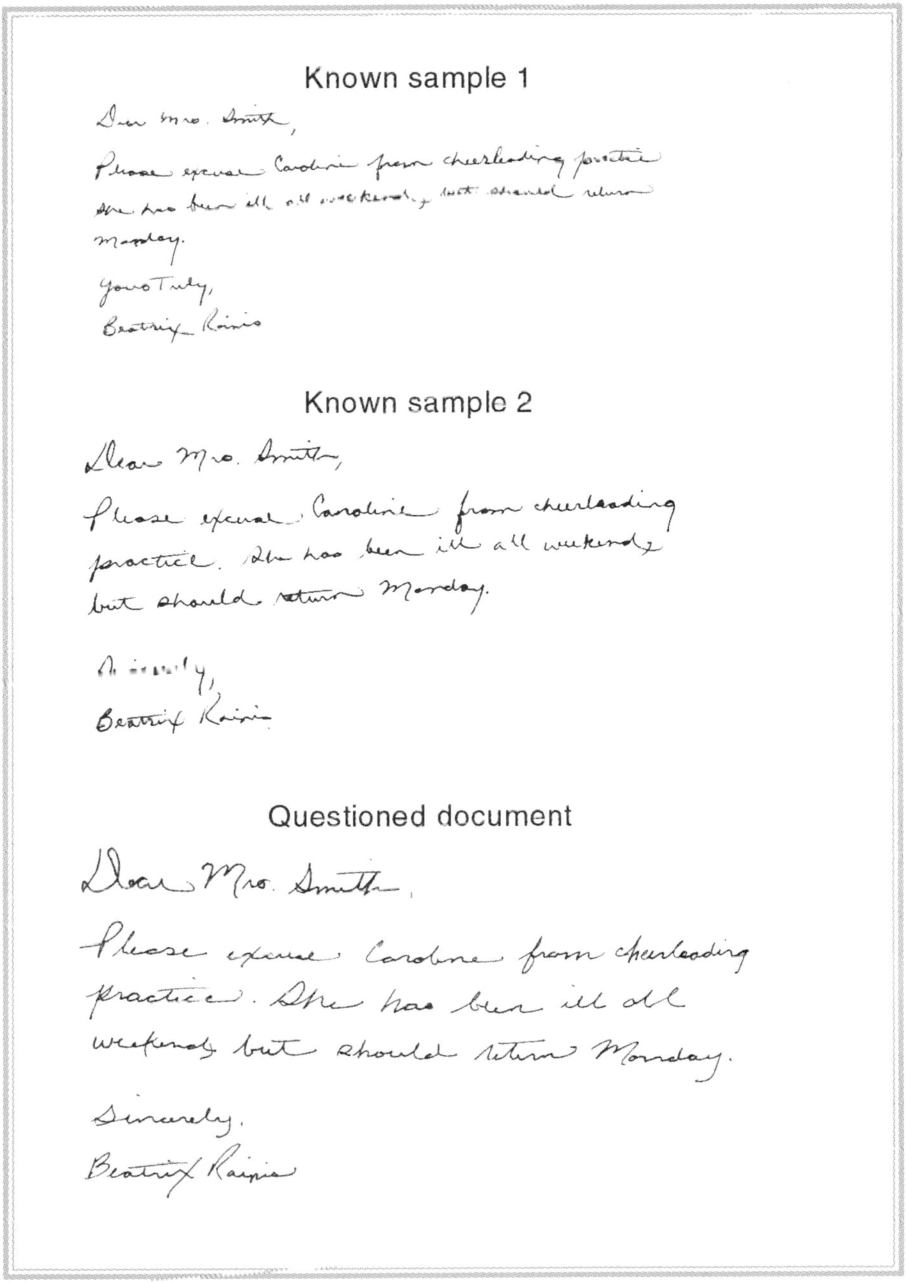

Known sample 1

[handwritten note]

Dear Mrs. Smith,

Please excuse Caroline from cheerleading practice
She has been ill all weekend, but should return
Monday.

Yours Truly,
Beatrix Rainis

Known sample 2

[handwritten note]

Dear Mrs. Smith,

Please excuse Caroline from cheerleading
practice. She has been ill all weekend
but should return Monday.

Sincerely,
Beatrix Rainis

Questioned document

[handwritten note]

Dear Mrs. Smith,

Please excuse Caroline from cheerleading
practice. She has been ill all
weekend but should return Monday.

Sincerely,
Beatrix Rainis

Figure 10. Compare the "questioned document" to "known" writing samples.

documents are written by the same person or there is a forgery along with five authentic samples. Have your friend identify the five original samples in the set when it is turned over to you for analysis. Your task is to determine whether the sixth document is a forgery.

Make careful drawings and notes in your notebook of the characteristic features of individual letters in the five genuine handwriting samples. For example, look at all the *t*s and *a*s. Make note of how much they vary in the five authentic samples.

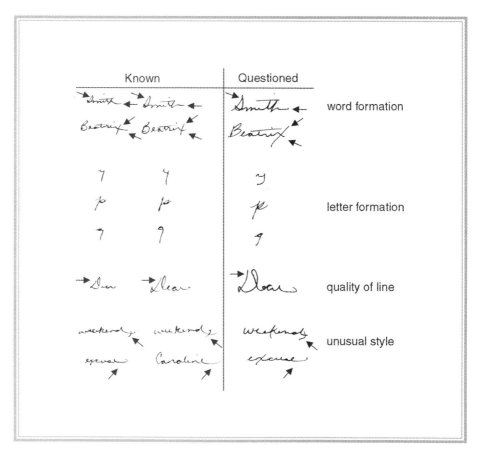

Figure 11. The "questioned" document is a forgery, as this analysis demonstrates.

Continue for as many letters as you like. Then, compare these known examples of letter formation to corresponding letters in the questioned document.

For your science project presentation, use the following analysis steps:

- Make a photocopy of the compared documents.

- Using Figure 11 and the checklist as a guide, select individual letters containing the comparison letters or words in both form and formation.

- Arrange the individual letters in a comparison table for known vs. unknown. Known is the authentic documents and unknown is the sixth document.

- Based upon your comparison analysis, is the sixth document in the set a forgery? Are the general pen movements (form) and the fine detail (formation) consistent among the five authentic letters?

Your analysis and conclusions (your expert opinion) should be included in your report. Have your friend confirm the authenticity of the sixth document in the set.

Science Projects You Can Do

Investigate the effect of age on chirography (penmanship).

Find a friend or relative who has lengthy writing samples, such as book reports, from the fourth grade, seventh grade, and ninth grade. Obtain two authentic samples (more if possible) from each time period. Make a detailed comparison of each of the documents and create a poster report that details, through a comparison table, similarities and differences in letter form and formation over this formative five-year period.

Examine whether the gender of the writer can be determined from an examination of handwriting.

Have a friend collect submitted written samples from classmates and friends. He or she should accumulate at least 10 documents from girls and 10 from boys. Writers should be from a similar age group. Have your friend keep a log of each document by number. The log should also record the gender of the author of each document. First, review documents in one group, making notes in your notebook concerning common characteristics among all submitted group samples. In a similar manner, review documents from the other group. Create a comparison table that illustrates the similarities in form and formation in each group.

Then have a friend collect writing samples from different people (people not in the original two groups but of the same age). You should not know if the new samples are from a male or female. After analyzing the samples, can you determine whether a male or female submitted them? Try performing this same type of analysis to determine right- or left-handedness.

Investigation 4.7

Looking at Paper Fiber

Materials

* fine stationery writing paper
* newspaper
* black construction paper
* magnifying glass, 10–15X
* microscope
* paper punch
* cup
* water
* tweezers
* microscope slides
* sharp toothpicks

Try to locate individual fiber classes, such as rag and wood, by examining a piece of fine stationery writing paper and a piece of newsprint. A wood fiber generally resembles a toothpick in shape. A rag fiber looks like a flat ribbon.

Examine dry paper fibers by carefully tearing a small piece of newspaper and placing its torn edge against black construction paper (to provide contrast). Use a 10–15X magnifying glass to see individual fibers. An average wood fiber is 3.5 mm (0.138 in) long and about 0.06 mm (0.024 in) in diameter.

If possible, next examine paper fibers under a microscope by making a wet mount. Use Figure 12 as a guide in examining paper fiber. Use a paper punch to stamp out a test circle from a piece of stationery paper. Soak the disk in a cup of water overnight. Use fine-point tweezers to remove the disk and place it in a drop of water on a clean microscope slide. Use sharp toothpicks to further separate individual fibers. Under a magnifying glass, use tweezers to pick up individual paper fibers and transfer them to another drop of water on another clean microscope slide. Add a coverslip and examine

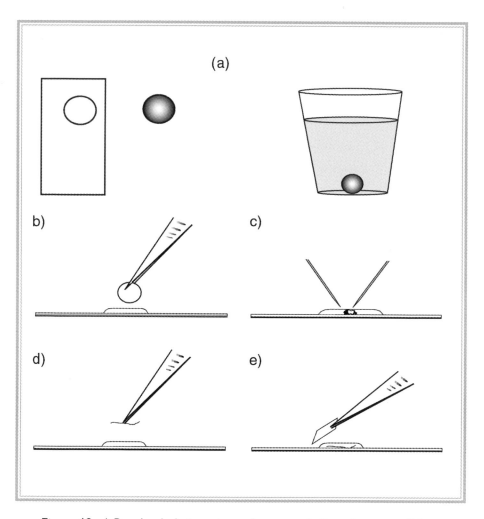

Figure 12. a) Punch a hole in a piece of paper and allow the paper disk to soften in water. b) Use tweezers to place the paper disk in a drop of water on a microscope slide; c) use sharp toothpicks to separate fibers. d) Use tweezers to remove individual fibers. e) Make a wet mount of separated fibers.

the fibers under 40X then 100X magnification. (Appendix A has information about using microscopes.)

You can determine fiber content of paper through microscopic examination. To estimate the percentage of fiber type (rag or wood) that has been used, tear a sheet of paper in such a way that individual fibers are exposed. Use tweezers to pick up 15 to 20 dry fibers at random. Prepare a wet mount sample and examine random fibers under a microscope. Use Figure 13 as a guide in identifying the fiber type. Determine the fiber content by dividing a particular fiber type count by the total number of fibers observed in the sample.

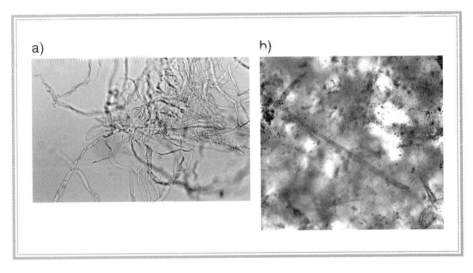

Figure 13. a) Rag and b) wood paper fibers.

Investigation 4.8

A Reference Collection of Papers

Materials

* various paper types, such as photocopying paper, checkout tape, fine-quality, and hand-made papers

* notebook

* Table 4-2

Examine various paper types ranging from inexpensive commercial photocopying and checkout tape papers to fine-quality and handmade papers such as watercolor papers. In your notebook, create a data table that characterizes each paper sample. Use Table 4-2 as your guide.

A Science Project You Can Do

Determine the age of newsprint.

Poor-quality paper yellows. Study the yellowing process by placing various paper samples in direct sunlight for a long time (four to eight weeks or longer). Do you notice yellowing? What do you see under a magnifying glass? Can you find individual fibers coated with lignin (woody component of plants) that are yellow or brownish yellow? What kind of light causes the fastest yellowing—the ultraviolet rays in sunlight or its other spectral colors? (Try using colored cellophane to filter the light.) Will incandescent or fluorescent lighting cause quicker newsprint yellowing?

Experiment with methods to slow down the yellowing process. Try dipping some small pieces of newsprint in a glass of water containing 2 teaspoons of borax (sodium borate) and allowing them to dry. Do these treated pieces yellow as quickly? What about those treated in vinegar?

TABLE 4-2. CHARACTERIZING PAPER SAMPLES

Characteristic	Comments
Manufacturer	Record if known. Make sure it is the manufacturer, not the distributor.
Size	Research the standard sizes for commercially prepared papers as well as specialty papers including fine watercolor papers.
Color	Research what colors are most frequently used by paper manufacturers. Is white really white?
Fluorescence properties	Use a common ultraviolet or black light (254–365 mm wavelength) to view paper samples under dark conditions. UV light reveals the presence of optical brighteners and other additives. Record emission results. (A fluorescent object is sensitive to ultraviolet light and will absorb the light energy. After a little while the object will release this energy in the form of visible light, which makes the object look like it is glowing.)
Sizing	The addition of starch or gelatin to paper so that inks will not bleed or absorb into the paper. It is either present or absent. You can find out by resting the point of the pen on the paper's surface and observing if the paper acts as blotting paper.
Fiber content	Based upon microscopic analysis, per Investigation 4.7.
Watermark	Photograph or illustrate the mark, if any (see Appendix A). Note date(s).

Casebook: Case of the Altered Photocopy

The photocopied letter below is submitted by a Miss Georgia Carpenter to your client as proof that the historical notebook she is offering for sale is genuine. The notebook is the actual minutes book of the trial of Major John André, a coconspirator with Benedict Arnold for the betrayal of West Point in Tappan, New York, in 1780. Your client knows that the signature of Lawson Burton, an expert in Revolutionary War documents, is genuine, but he suspects that the document may have been altered. He has decided to submit the document to you for expert verification. Conduct your analysis and write your report.

```
                          Lawson Burton
                          45 Crossover Road
                          Fairport, NY  14450

Dear Ms. Carpenter:

This letter will confirm that on April 1, 1998, I examined the notebook
manuscript of trial minutes kept by a Captain Jenjins, adjutant to General
George Washington, regarding the trial of Major John Andre of the British
army.

Based upon my direct examination of the manuscript as well as the provenance
detail you have provided, I conclude that this historic document is genuine.
Thank you for the opportunity to review this interesting document.


Sincerely yours,

Lawson Burton
Rare Manuscript Authority
Micrographia
```

Figure 14. Determine if this photocopied document has been altered.

Chapter 5

Counterfeiting and Forgery

A printing press—a counterfeiter's outfit.

—Sherlock Holmes

Counterfeiting is the unauthorized duplication of an object. With digital technology, printing expertise is not needed for someone to counterfeit documents. To combat the threat of counterfeiting, new printing and other techniques have been created.

The art of forgery is as old as the alphabet; it is the deliberate changing of a document for the purpose of deceit or fraud. Any ink-on-paper document can be forged. There is never anything like the "perfect forgery," however, because the change is in itself a marker for the careful eye to discover.

Investigation 5.1

Security Audits

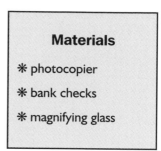

Materials

* photocopier

* bank checks

* magnifying glass

An audit is a careful review. You can perform a security audit on a bank check. Ask an adult for permission to examine a blank check from a neighborhood bank. Use Tables 5-1 and 5-2 and Figure 15 as guides in conducting your security audit.

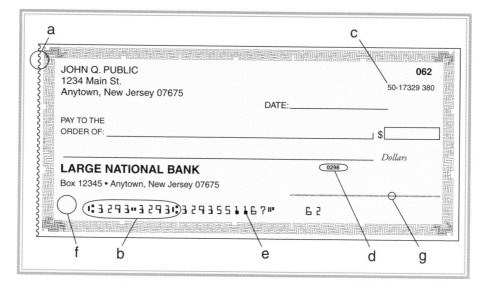

Figure 15. Compare a check from a local bank with this diagram. a) Perforations on at least one side. b) The nine-place number is the routing code for the bank the check is drawn on. The first two digits represent the Federal Reserve District Number. c) A routing fraction appears at the upper right. It is important that you compare the number to the full routing code. Forgers will sometimes change these numbers in order to gain more "float time" by first causing the check to be routed to another bank before finally being presented to the correct bank for payment. d) Date code when check was printed. e) Magnetic ink used to print numbers. f) Laid lines— these challenge cutting and pasting. g) Microdot printing is usually used as a signature line.

TABLE 5-1. SECURITY FEATURES OF CHECKS

Security Feature	Comment
Perforations	You should be able to feel perforations on at least one edge of any legitimate check. (Certain government checks, such as Department of the Treasury checks, do not have perforations.)
Federal Reserve District Number Designation	This two-digit number indicates in which of the twelve Federal Reserve Districts the bank is located. This number should agree with the routing code printed at the upper right portion of a legitimate check. (See Table 5-2.)
Magnetic Numbers	Automatic check sorting machines require special (and restricted) magnetic ink. This ink has a flat or dull appearance when viewed under normal lighting conditions. If you spot a shine or reflection off these numbers when viewing a bank check under normal lighting, it is not a legitimate check or is a forgery.
Microprinting	Printed words or phrases so small that if photocopied they appear as a solid line.
Security Screen	A printed graphic containing a word or words that disappear if the document is photocopied.
Pantograph	Colored print area that displays VOID if photocopied.
High-resolution Latent Images	Hidden letters or images concealed within the overall document design.
Fluorescent Inks	Visible only under a black light
Chemical Protection	Stains, spots, or VOID can be seen directly or when held up to direct lighting, signaling that a portion of the check has been chemically altered—application of a hypochlorite or bleach solution to chemically remove dye-based inks.
Laid Lines	Closely spaced parallel lines on the document to challenge cutting and pasting.

TABLE 5-2. FEDERAL RESERVE BANK CODES

01	Massachusetts, Maine, New Hampshire, Connecticut, Vermont, Rhode Island
02	New York, New Jersey, Connecticut
03	Pennsylvania, Delaware, New Jersey
04	Ohio, Pennsylvania, Kentucky, West Virginia
05	Virginia; Maryland; North Carolina; Washington, D.C.; South Carolina; West Virginia
06	Georgia, Alabama, Florida, Tennessee, Louisiana, Mississippi
07	Illinois, Michigan, Indiana, Iowa, Wisconsin
08	Missouri, Arkansas, Kentucky, Tennessee, Indiana, Illinois, Mississippi
09	Minnesota, Montana, North Dakota, South Dakota, Wisconsin, Michigan
10	Missouri, Colorado, Oklahoma, Nebraska, Iowa, Wyoming, Kansas, New Mexico
11	Texas, Arizona, New Mexico, Louisiana
12	California, Oregon, Washington, Idaho, Utah, Alaska, Hawaii, Nevada, Arizona

Examine the check for some of the items listed in Table 5-1. Then, with adult permission, test the effectiveness of several security features of the checks.

Visit a bank near you and interview the branch manager. Learn how banks and other financial institutions monitor the security features in Table 5-1 for forgery. Find out if the bank uses more than one check printing company for its clients' checks. If possible, compare security features for bank checks with those of other check printing services—checks tied to home computer check writing programs, for example. Determine if there are any major security feature differences.

Based on your audits, identify the most effective security features—those that provide readily visible evidence of attempted forgery. Prepare a poster that illustrates your findings. Can you think of other security features that could also be used?

A Science Project You Can Do

How effective is microprinting?

Microprinting is a printed word or phrase so small that if photocopied, it appears as a solid line. Identify microprinting areas on a bank check. With adult permission, photocopy the blank check and observe and record what occurs. Is the security feature more or less effective if color copies are made? Try different photocopier machines. Are the newer models less effective against this security measure than models that have been in use for many years?

Investigation 5.2

Chemistry as a Security Measure

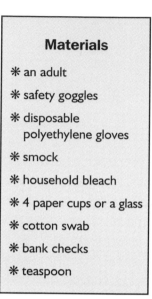

Materials

* an adult

* safety goggles

* disposable
  polyethylene gloves

* smock

* household bleach

* 4 paper cups or a glass

* cotton swab

* bank checks

* teaspoon

Do this investigation under adult supervision. **CAUTION: Bleach solutions can cause chemical burns! Use eye and hand protection.** Wear chemical safety goggles, protective hand wear (disposable polyethylene gloves), and a smock when working with bleach solutions.

Sometimes forgers use bleach solutions to chemically erase inks so that a signature or check amount can be altered. Bank checks and other similar documents use protective chemicals that show when a bleaching agent has been applied.

Carefully pour a few drops of household bleach into a small cup. Dip a cotton swab into the bleach solution and then rub it onto an area of a blank check, as shown in Figure 16. Allow the solution to dry.

Record your observations. Can you determine what is reacting with the bleach solution? Is it the printing inks or the paper?

Pour a teaspoon of bleach into another paper cup, and add a teaspoon of water. Use another cotton swab to apply this diluted solution to another similar area of a blank check. Do you observe similar results?

Try applying various other dilutions of bleach solution on other selected check areas. Find out how sensitive the alteration

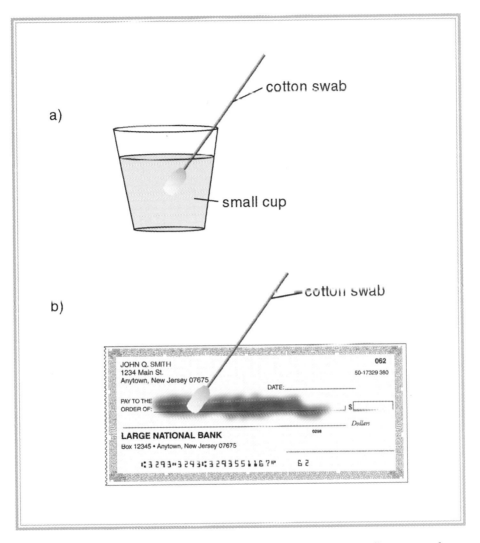

a)

cotton swab

small cup

b)

cotton swab

JOHN Q. SMITH
1234 Main St.
Anytown, New Jersey 07675

062

50-17329 380

DATE:

PAY TO THE
ORDER OF:

$

Dollars

LARGE NATIONAL BANK
Box 12345 • Anytown, New Jersey 07675

0298

⑈3293⑈3293⑈3293551167⑈   62

Figure 16. CAUTION: Put on safety goggles. a) Pour a small amount of bleach into a small cup. b) Wet a cotton swab in the bleach solution and apply it over an area of a blank check.

feature is. Express the concentration of bleach you use in parts per million (ppm). Household bleach is approximately 5 percent, or 50,000 ppm. A dilution of 1 part bleach to 3 parts water would give you a 1.25 percent (12,500 ppm) solution. Generally, this security feature is sensitive to bleach solutions greater than 0.1 percent or 1,000 ppm.

Concentrations as Percents and Parts per Million	
10%	100,000 ppm
1%	10,000 ppm
0.1%	1,000 ppm
0.01%	100 ppm
0.001%	10 ppm
0.0001%	1 ppm

Science Projects You Can Do

View fluorescent inks in a whole different light.

A fluorescent object is sensitive to ultraviolet light and absorbs this invisible light energy. The object releases this energy in the form of visible light, which makes the object glow.

Obtain a common black lightbulb from a party goods store. With adult permission, pass a blank bank check in front of the black light. Do you observe the presence of special fluorescent inks or embedded fibers?

Compare security features of the new Series 1996 U.S. currency with previous series issued between 1990 and 1995.

The new Series 1996 U.S. currency notes incorporate enhanced security features that protect against advanced digital technology counterfeiting. If possible, examine all three note denominations—$100, $50, and $20—from the new U.S. series and those from a year between 1990 and 1995. Use Table 5-3 to locate particular security features on each note denomination. Are any Series 1996 security features present in any earlier (1990–1995) series banknotes of similar denomination? Create a poster that illustrates the position of particular security features in new versus old currency.

In the United States, the most counterfeited denomination is the $20 note, followed by the $100 note, the $10 note, the $50 note, the $1 note, and the $5 note.

The Secret Service, the federal agency charged with investigating counterfeiting, maintains a special forensic science laboratory that includes:

- a complete library of banknote specimens dating from 1865;

- the largest collection of watermark files in existence;

- the largest ink library in existence; and

- equipment to examine and analyze notes counterfeited by a wide variety of devices, ranging from printing presses to digital color copiers.

TABLE 5-3. U.S. SERIES 1996 BANKNOTE SECURITY FEATURES

Security Feature	Comment
1 Portrait (engraved image)	Enlarged portrait is easy to recognize for visually impaired; off-center placement.
2 Concentric Fine Lines	Fine parallel lines are difficult to duplicate.
3 Watermark	A watermark depicting the portrait is visible from both sides when held up to the light. It does not copy on color printers.
4 Color-shifting Ink	Ink looks black when viewed straight on, but appears green when viewed at an angle.
5 Microprinting	Tiny printing in many locations on the front of the note. Clearly visible with a magnifier. The resolution of most current copiers is not sufficient to copy such fine print.
6 Security Thread	Vertical imprinted polyester thread can be seen from both sides when held up to a light. Thread glows red or green under a black light. Cannot be reproduced in the reflected light of copiers.
7 Paper and Fibers	Cotton and linen rag paper; tiny red and blue fibers embedded in the paper.
8 Treasury Seal	The sawtooth points are sharp and unbroken. Seal's color is the same as the two serial numbers.
9 Serial Numbers	A unique combination of 11 numbers and letters is printed in two places on the front of the note. These numbers are evenly spaced with ink the same color as the treasury seal. No two notes of the same series and denomination have the same serial number.
10 Federal Reserve Seal	A new universal seal represents the entire Federal Reserve system.

Investigation 5.3

Signature Duplicators

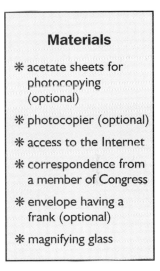

Materials

* acetate sheets for photocopying (optional)
* photocopier (optional)
* access to the Internet
* correspondence from a member of Congress
* envelope having a frank (optional)
* magnifying glass

Favorites of the modern forger are signatures of past presidents, most notably Abraham Lincoln. It is estimated that Lincoln's letters and documents are more often forged than those of any other person in history. Lincoln's handwriting changed little during his lifetime. Other presidents, such as George Washington, John F. Kennedy, and Richard Nixon, altered their handwriting considerably during their careers. Figure 17 shows two signatures of President Richard Nixon.

One Nixon signature is authentic. There are two characteristics that authentic signatures of Nixon almost always have. They lack a second *r* in *Richard*, and the *d* is lower than the *R*. Secretarial signatures (signatures authorized by an individual but still not genuine) have always put in the *r* and made the *d* the highest part of the *Richard*. This is often termed "the proud d" by Nixon autograph experts. So which one is the authentic signature?

Many individuals who write a lot of letters or who are sought after for their signature often employ a mechanical device called an autopen to create it. Some forensic experts regard these mechanical signatures as being in between a genuine signature and a forgery. Most professional autograph

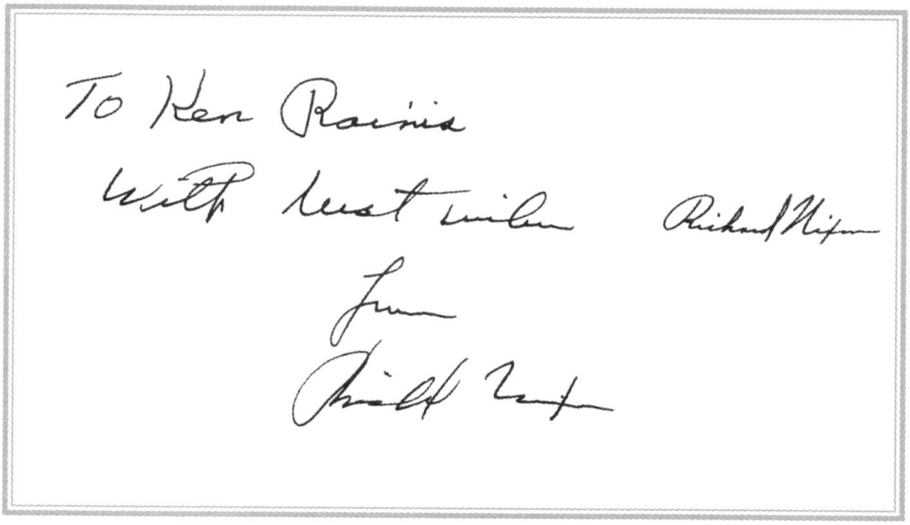

Figure 17. Richard Nixon signatures

collectors call these mechanical signatures "patterns," since the machine follows a pattern. Every president since John F. Kennedy has routinely used the device.

Autopen patterns are easy to spot. An autopen machine holds the pen at a 90-degree angle, making every stroke the same width. Humans hold the pen at a different angle, making different widths in pen writing or printing strokes. Also, autopens cannot make curves. Under a magnifying glass you will observe a series of short, straight lines that simulate a curve.

Visit the Web site of an autograph dealer (search under "signature, autopen"). Dealers will usually display autopen patterns that you can observe. Since no two signatures will match exactly, signatures that do are most likely created by a machine following a pattern. At the Web site, print out Web pages displaying autopen signatures. Photocopy these patterns onto transparent acetate sheets. Place the acetate sheets over each other and inspect for an identical match—an autopen pattern. Autograph dealers routinely do this to detect autopen signatures in collections they acquire.

Members of Congress and past presidents have a "franking" privilege of free mailing for letters involving official correspondence; their signature is their official mark, or frank. Until the nineteenth century it was common for presidents and members of Congress to sign the corner of the envelope as a free postage frank. Most franks today are electronic signatures made by computers.

Write to your federal representative (senator or congressman) and explain that you are conducting an investigation into autopen signatures. Ask that they forward as many of their signatures as they can provide. Chances are extremely good that you will end up with replies that contain signatures that appear identical.

Perform the following review of these signatures:

- Confirm that the patterns are identical by placing two identical-looking signatures over each other and holding them up to the light.

- Autopen patterns will be completely uniform in thickness and pressure. Use a magnifying glass to confirm these characteristics.

- Autopen patterns will often look shaky.

Casebook: Case of the Rare Autographs

Gerry wanted to own some authentic celebrity autographs, or even a presidential signature. The local autograph dealer said that he had just purchased a collection from a former U.S. senator that contained many documents bearing the signature of President Bill Clinton and that of his personal friend, famed baseball player Mickey Mantle. The dealer claimed that all the signatures were very rare. Gerry has asked you to evaluate them.

You know the following information from knowledgeable collectors: the president often signs *Bill Clinton* or *Bill* on correspondence and other nonofficial items. Frequently, if he is rushed, *Bill Clinton* appears to be written as one word, though his desk signatures generally appear as two distinct words. He usually reserves *William J. Clinton* for official documents.

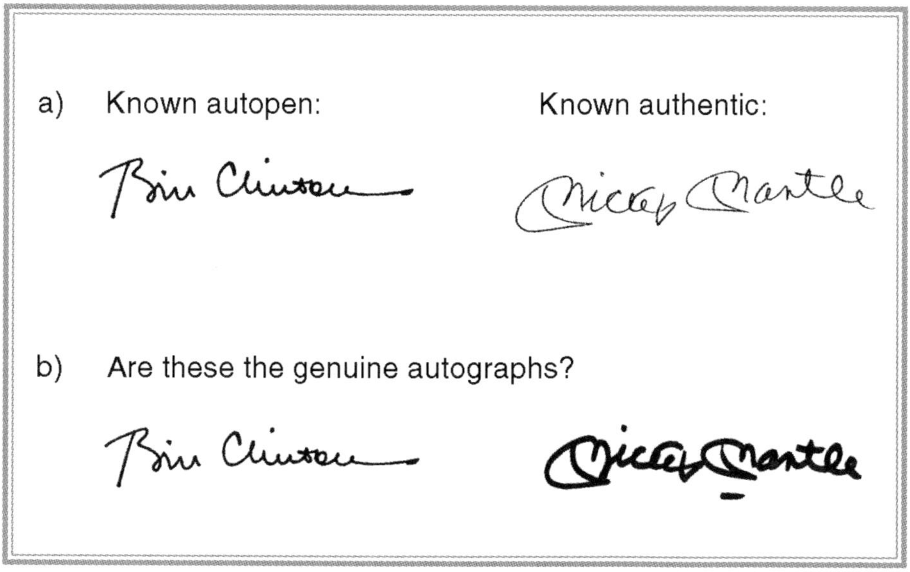

a) Known autopen: Known authentic:

b) Are these the genuine autographs?

Figure 18. a) Known autopen pattern of Bill Clinton and a known authentic autograph of Mickey Mantle. b) Would you advise your client to purchase these autographs as genuine?

Chapter 6

Blood Evidence

Are they blood stains, or mud stains, or rust stains, or fruit stains, or what are they? That is a question which has puzzled many an expert . . .

—Sherlock Holmes

Examining blood can provide the forensic scientist with a wealth of information in many areas of a criminal investigation. Blood evidence can include bloodstain patterns that can often "describe" the crime scene. Various biochemical tests are used by forensic investigators to identify the source of the blood found at a crime scene and, if human, the blood type.

Since 1985, forensic scientists have been able to describe the genetic makeup of an individual based upon the DNA recovered from blood and other body fluids and tissues. In 1994 the FBI developed the Combined DNA Identification System (CODIS). The FBI shares DNA information about incarcerated individuals with other law enforcement agencies. It is hoped that this new system can match DNA from earlier, unrelated cases.

Investigation 6.1

Is It Blood?

At times, a crime scene investigator will come upon an unidentified dry stain. Is it rust, shoe polish, fruit juice, or dried blood? There is a quick and sensitive chemical test that detects an enzyme (peroxidase) in the blood. Peroxidase is found in most plant cells and some animal cells, including blood cells. In blood, this enzyme helps get oxygen to body tissues. The peroxidase test is used by forensic laboratory technicians to test for the presence of blood.

Carry out this test under adult supervision, and **wear safety goggles and polyethylene gloves. The phenolphthalein solution is flammable; avoid contact with any open flame or hot surface. Do not use human blood.**

> **Materials**
>
> * an adult
> * safety goggles
> * disposable polyethylene gloves
> * animal blood from packaged meats
> * test fluids: food colorings, theatrical makeup
> * absorbent pieces of cotton cloth
> * pencil
> * paper toweling
> * 2 eyedroppers or pipettes
> * phenolphthalein solution
> * hydrogen peroxide solution (3%)

Have an adult apply drops of non-blood fluids and drops of animal blood from packaged meats to pieces of cotton cloth (such as from a handkerchief). Allow these fluid stains to dry. Use a pencil to number the cloth pieces.

To carry out the test, rub a piece of dry paper toweling on the suspected stain. Using an eyedropper, carefully apply drops of phenolphthalein solution to the rubbed area of paper towel. Use a different eyedropper to apply drops of 3 percent hydrogen peroxide over the same area. A positive result for blood is the immediate appearance of a pink color along with some foaming on the rubbed-off trace. The peroxidase test will also provide a strong reaction with traces of blood too small to be seen. A negative result (no pink and no foaming) indicates the complete absence of blood. Can you correctly identify which numbered cloth piece(s) contained bloodstains?

A Science Project You Can Do

Explore false positives and other matters.

The peroxidase blood test can produce false positives—meaning that when the test chemicals are added, a pink color along with foaming results even when the fluid is not blood. The reason is that other peroxidases (plant and animal) are present in the suspect stain. For example, a green vegetable smear may produce a positive test result.

Learn more about the peroxidase reaction. Visit your school library or check out peroxidase enzymes on the Internet. Create a data table that records peroxidase test results from various natural substances: fruit juices, tree saps, and other plant fluids that can cause a stain. Apply these substances on pieces of paper toweling and allow them to dry. Record which substances show a foaming (positive) reaction following the application of the test solutions.

Hint: Investigate what happens if you test a stain created from crushed fresh horseradish root (loaded with peroxidase!) mixed in a tablespoon of red fruit juice.

Test if warm temperatures and extended time periods (days, weeks) affect peroxidase test results on previously positive test substances. Do positive tests develop more slowly?

Investigation 6.2

Formulating Simulated Blood

Materials

* measuring cup

* tablespoon

* cornstarch

* water

* corn syrup

* teaspoon

* green and red food coloring

* white glue

In a measuring cup mix 4 tablespoons of cornstarch thoroughly with ⅔ cup of water. Add ⅔ cup of corn syrup and mix well.

Place 3 teaspoons of the mixture in a dish and add 3 to 5 drops of red food coloring. Then add a few drops of green food coloring to reduce the pinkish coloration of the mixture.

If the mixture is too light, add one or two drops more of red food coloring. Add an extra drop of green food coloring if the mixture gets too pink again. (Real blood is dark red to reddish brown.)

Add the white glue, starting with about 1 or 2 teaspoons, to keep the mixture from becoming too transparent—a common fault with fake blood. Use the teaspoon to mix well. Check flowability by stirring and rapidly raising the teaspoon. A good batch of fake blood has a heavy, watery look as it is stirred. Add additional corn syrup or white glue, as needed, to even out the entire effect.

Investigating Blood Droplets and Bloodstains

When a drop of blood separates from its source, physical forces—viscosity (resistance to flow), surface tension (the ability to form a surface layer), and gravity—affect it. These forces influence both the size of the drop as well as its path. Experiments have shown that the average volume of a drop of blood is approximately 0.05 mL.

A Science Project You Can Do

What shape does a blood droplet take?

You can study how the forces of surface tension and gravity affect a droplet of blood. After you have made simulated blood, set up white poster board. Use a camera with a flash to photograph drops of simulated blood falling through a vertical distance of at least three feet.

Use your finger as a wick by dipping it in the fake blood and then allowing drops of it to form and fall off your finger. This action simulates a finger cut. Drops must fall a distance greater than three feet for there to be enough time for gravity to display its effect on the drop. Enlist the aid of a volunteer photographer. Be sure that the camera can focus on the colored drop, which will contrast with the white poster board backdrop. Have the drop images enlarged as much as possible by the photo developer. Use a magnifying glass to observe the outline of the drop. What can you conclude about the shape of a falling blood droplet from viewing these photographs?

Investigation 6.3

Determining the Fall Angle and Height from Bloodstain Shapes

By looking at bloodstain shapes, you can figure out the fall angle and height from which the blood fell. First you will need to make a bloodstain database for comparison.

Cover a table with a plastic drop cloth. Allow a single drop of simulated blood (that you made in Investigation 6.2) to form and fall from an eyedropper onto a 6-in white cardboard square. The dropper should be held 6 inches above the card. For each drop, use a different square and vary the tilt of the square. Use a protractor and some supports to create the various impact angles: 90°, 80°, 70°, 60°, 50°, 40°, 30°, 20°, and 10°. Use Figure 19 as a guide. Repeat the experiment from a height of 12 inches, 4 feet, and 8 feet onto separate cards. (**Have an adult present when you are dropping simulated blood from a height greater than 4 feet.**) Allow the simulated blood droplet to dry. Use a pencil to write the information (impact angle, drop distance) concerning the drop test on the lower right corner of each cardboard square. Keep the cardboard squares as visual guides for future investigations. Based upon your blood-drop studies, can you write a general

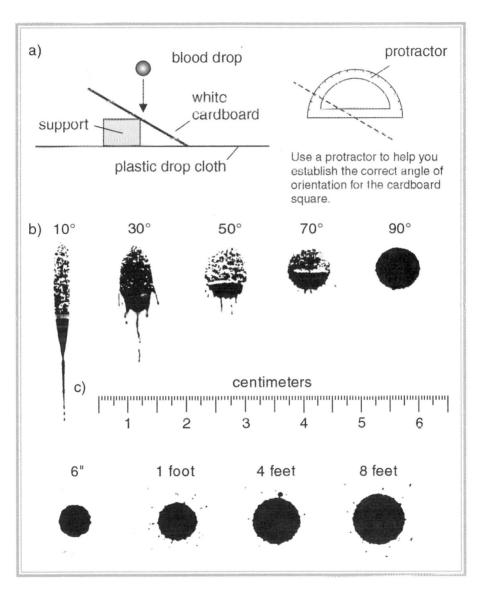

Figure 19. a) Setup to capture bloodstain profiles. b) Shape of bloodstains relative to an increasing angle of impact of single blood drops from an eyedropper allowed to fall onto smooth white cardboard. c) Increasing diameter of bloodstains as a function of increasing distance by single drops allowed to fall onto smooth white cardboard.

prediction concerning impact droplet shapes occurring at various impact angles and drop distances?

Conduct additional blood-drop studies to learn more about the following:

- Does the fall distance of a free-falling drop affect its shape or diameter?

- Does surface type (textured or rough versus smooth) affect drop shape?

Investigation 6.4

Predicting Blood Splash Patterns

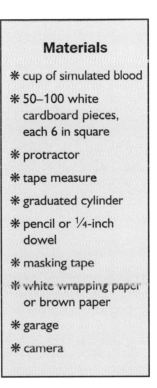

Materials

* cup of simulated blood
* 50–100 white cardboard pieces, each 6 in square
* protractor
* tape measure
* graduated cylinder
* pencil or ¼-inch dowel
* masking tape
* white wrapping paper or brown paper
* garage
* camera

When more than 1 mL of blood impacts a surface, a splash pattern will result. These patterns play a critical role in determining the position of a victim and the assailant during an assault.

Use your finger as a wick by dipping it in simulated blood (that you made in Investigation 6.2) and then allowing single drops to form and fall. Repeat as many variables described in Investigation 6.3 as possible. Create a card file to record your results. Analyze your results to address these questions:

- How are impact splash patterns related to impact angles?

- Does surface type (textured or rough versus smooth) affect the splash pattern?

- Are splash patterns changed as increasingly greater volumes (2 mL, 3 mL) are used?

Castoff bloodstain patterns are produced when blood flies off a blunt object, such as a bloody weapon in motion.

Make sure you have adult permission to continue with this part of the project—even fake bloodstains are not easy to clean up!

Use a pencil or ¼-inch dowel as the blunt object. Tape white wrapping paper on a garage wall and floor. Use your finger to coat the "weapon" with simulated blood. Devise various striking poses that answer the questions below. Remember to use clean sheets of paper for each strike pose and to label the papers. Document the pose using a camera. You may want to construct multiple story lines to support your hypothesis.

- How does the splash pattern indicate the direction of travel?

- Which type of strike movement creates more castoffs—downswings or upswings?

- Is there a relationship between stain shape and the distance the drops traveled?

Casebook: Case of the Bloodstained Pavement

No body has yet been found, but there is a missing-person report on file for a young woman who was last observed in the area. You are a bloodstain expert. You are to determine if the bloodstains on sidewalk pavement stones shown in Figure 20 are castoffs from a bloody blunt weapon or simply drips of blood. The suspect states that he injured himself while using a sickle to trim grass along the edge of the pavement. Analyze the evidence and write your report.

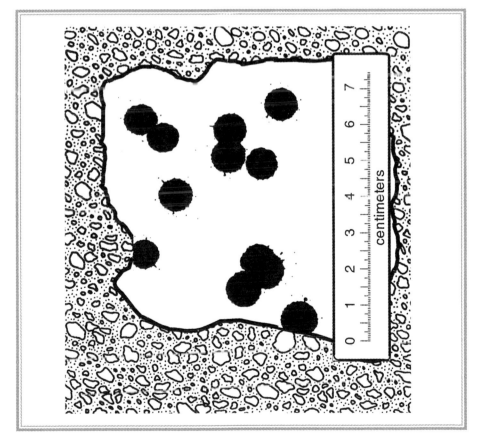

Figure 20. A representation of blood splatters on the sidewalk pavement.

Chapter 7

Trace Evidence

There is as much difference between the black ash of a Trichinopoly [a type of cigar made from tobacco grown in Trichinopoly, India] and the white fluff of a bird's eye as there is between a cabbage and a potato.

—Sherlock Holmes

Chapter 2 introduced an important part of forensic science—physical evidence. As you learned, physical evidence can be either in large or in trace amounts. Edmond Locard (1877–1966), a French criminologist, believed that individuals could not enter an area without taking dust particles with them from the crime scene. Locard's principle is: Every contact leaves a trace.

Trace evidence is a branch of forensics that involves the examination and analysis of small particles. It helps establish a link between a suspect and a crime scene or a suspect and the victim of a crime. The majority of this particulate matter is fibers.

Fibers and Hairs

Fibers obtained from a plant or an animal are known as natural fibers. Synthetic fibers are made from chemical-based raw materials that are squeezed out through tiny holes under pressure to form threads.

Plant fibers come from the seed hairs, leaves and husks (the source of hard cordage fibers), and stems (the source of soft bast fibers) of the plant. Bast fibers are primarily used in weaving textiles, and the coarser cordage fibers are used for rope and twine. Animal fibers are provided, generally, by animal hair and, in the case of silk, by the secretion of the silkworm. Use the following guide to natural and synthetic fibers as a reference resource.

Natural and Synthetic Fibers

Use the "applied tape" or wet mount technique to view fibers under the microscope (40X); See Investigation 7.1.

Animal

Human

Cylindrical; the flatter the hair in cross section, the curlier it is. Made of three overlapping layers. The outermost (cuticle) is made of thin overlapping cells; the middle layer (cortex) is made of many elongated cells; the inner layer (medulla) is made of rectangular cells. Hair color (yellow to black) results mostly from a pigment (melanin) distributed within the cortex. Used in wigs.

Wool

Cylindrical, coiled. Grades (fiber diameter): Fine (17–22 μm), Medium (22–30 μm), Coarse (31–36 μm), Very Coarse (36–40 μm). NOTE: a micrometer (μm) = 0.000001 of a meter, or about 0.000039 inch. The shaft consists of a core of cortical cells enclosed by a cuticle of overlapping flattened cells in a scaly pattern, with free margins pointing toward the fiber's tip. Cortical cells are long, narrow, and cigar-shaped. Used in textiles and carpets.

Silk

cultivated silkworm, *Bombyx mori*

Filament 0.025 mm (0.001 inch); nearly triangular; reflective white (commercial) or brown and hairy (natural). Strongest of all natural fibers; resistant to heat and will burn only as long as a flame is applied to it. Silk is used in textiles.

Plant

Cotton

Gossypium species

Spiral twist; No other natural fiber has elasticity. Cotton is used in textiles and twine.

Flax

Linum usitatissimum

Cylindrical, long and hollow. One of the oldest cultivated plants. Cloth made from flax is called linen. Linen found among the remains of the Neolithic Swiss lake dwellers. Flax is used in table linens.

Synthetic

Rayon

Extruded filament; called artificial silk, it is produced from regenerated cellulose (wood pulp). Acetate and triacetate are rayon fibers that are chemical derivatives (esters) of cellulose. Rayon is used in clothing (long filament—triacetate rayon);

filling materials in pillows, mattress pads, quilts, and as filtering agents in cigarettes (short filament—acetate rayon).

Nylon

Cold-drawn (stretched), extruded, elastic filament. The shape of individual threads can be changed to refract or reflect light. Threads can be produced that contain linear voids along their entire length, creating interesting visual effects. Nylon is used in carpeting and pantyhose.

Polyester

Cold-drawn (stretched); hollow. Threads are stretched to produce the degree of strength and elasticity desired, then crimped, coiled, or otherwise textured before being woven or knitted into fabric. Polyester is used in lightweight clothing; insulation; water- and wind-resistant fabrics.

A Closer Look at Human Hair

Like the hair of all mammals, human hair grows from a hair follicle, a porelike organ within the skin. Hair is made up of two distinct parts: the shaft, or the portion that projects from the skin, which we see; and the root, which is inside the follicle deep within the skin. As Figure 21 shows, hair develops from cells of the hair bulb, which divide rapidly. These cells move upward as new cells begin to form beneath them. As these cells move away from the source of nourishment (tiny blood vessels), they start to form a hard protein called keratin. This process is called keratinization, and the hair dies as soon as this occurs.

Human hair is either terminal or vellus. Terminal hairs are usually long, coarse, and pigmented. They are found in the scalp and in some other body areas. Vellus hair is short, fine, and is found over much of the rest of the body. Scalp hairs

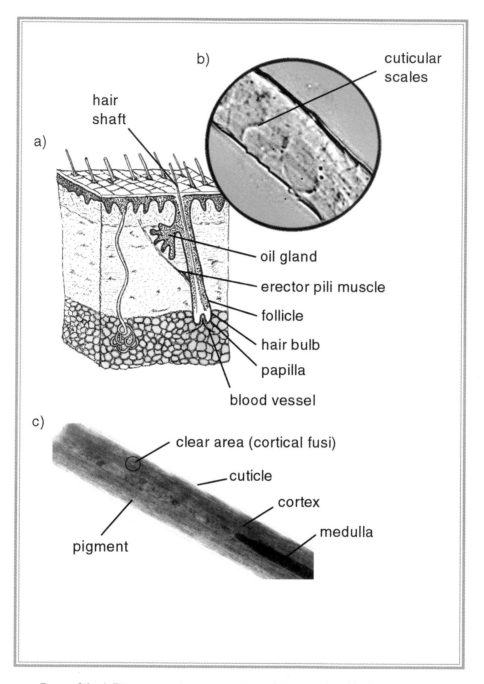

a) **hair shaft**, **oil gland**, **erector pili muscle**, **follicle**, **hair bulb**, **papilla**, **blood vessel**

b) **cuticular scales**

c) **clear area (cortical fusi)**, **cuticle**, **cortex**, **medulla**, **pigment**

Figure 21. a) Diagrammatic cross section of human skin. b) Cuticle scales; 640X. c) Human hair; 640X.

grow less than half an inch (13 mm) per month. Vellus hairs grow for about ten weeks and then rest for about nine months.

Hair is made of three distinct layers: cuticle, cortex, and medulla. The cuticle is the hard outside covering that protects the inner layers. It is made of overlapping scales.

Obtain a rather long strand of hair from your head and hold it by the root between your left forefinger and thumb. Gently draw the hair strand from the root to the tip, applying firm pressure, through the forefinger and thumb of your right hand. Now reverse the procedure, drawing the hair strand from tip to root. Which direction offers more resistance? The resistance you feel is due to the presence of thousands of cells that make up the outer layer of hair—the cuticle. These are laid down as overlapping scales with their edges pointing

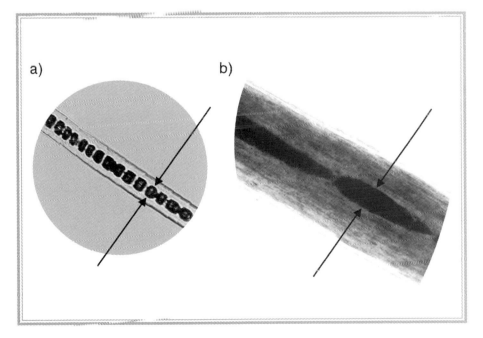

a) b)

Figure 22. a) Cat hair—medullary index 0.5; 320X. b) Human hair—medullary index 0.33; 640X.

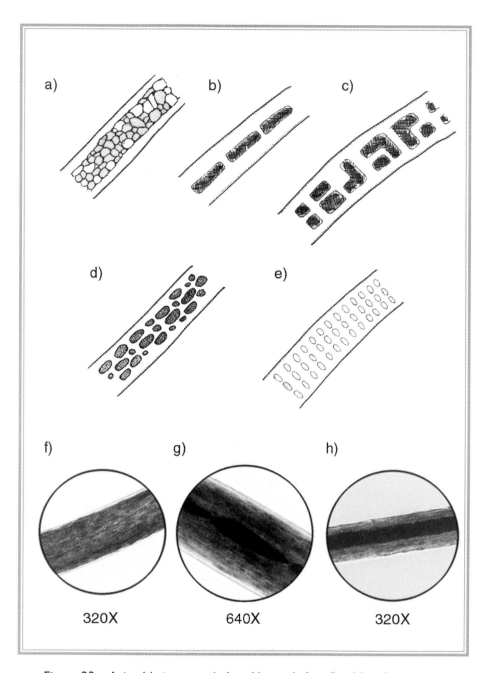

320X   640X   320X

Figure 23. *Animal hair types:* a) deer b) cat c) dog d) rabbit e) mouse. *Human hair types:* Caucasian and African American— f) medullary core absent, g) medullary core interrupted, Asian—h) medullary core continuous.

toward the tip. (Generally you need a microscope [at least 50X] to observe cuticle scales.)

Use this touch method to examine other hair types such as dog hair and wool.

A large portion (70 to 90 percent) of a human hair is composed of cortex. These cells contain the pigments that give hair its color. The medulla is made up of cells that run through the center of the cortex. In humans, this is a small-diameter canal that may be continuous, interrupted, fragmented, or in some cases absent. Forensic scientists determine the medullary index of hair—the relationship between the diameter of the medulla and the diameter of the hair—expressed as a fraction. For example, humans have a medullary value of less than $\frac{1}{3}$, or 0.33. Animal hair has a medullary index of greater than 0.50. Use Figures 22 and 23 to compare human and animal hairs. See Appendix A to learn about various microscopy techniques, including estimating the size of objects viewed under the microscope.

Sometimes race can be determined by the examination of hairs. Hairs of both African Americans and Caucasians have a medullary core that is either absent or interrupted. Hairs of individuals of Asian decent have a continuous medullary core. See Figure 23f–h.

Today, it is a common occurrence for hair color to be altered through bleaching or dyeing. Bleaching removes the pigment and gives hair a yellow tint. Dye can reach either the cuticle or cortex of a hair to change its color.

Investigation 7.1

Hair and Fiber Collection and Examination

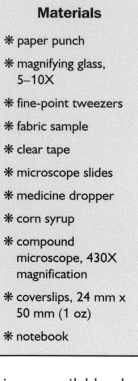

Materials

* paper punch
* magnifying glass, 5–10X
* fine-point tweezers
* fabric sample
* clear tape
* microscope slides
* medicine dropper
* corn syrup
* compound microscope, 430X magnification
* coverslips, 24 mm x 50 mm (1 oz)
* notebook

A forensic hair and fiber examiner recognizes, collects, and preserves physical, trace, and microscopic evidence. There are three main methods by which this is done.

1. Scientists protect clothing or other physical evidence at the scene by placing it in a labeled paper bag for later examination.

2. Scientists collect hair and fiber evidence using tweezers and place the evidence in small paper envelopes. (If an envelope is not available, they fold a sheet of paper and use tweezers to deposit the fiber on the fold. Then they fold the paper lengthwise again and the outer ends in on themselves.) They label the envelope and the evidence can then be safely transported to the laboratory for examination.

3. Scientists use clear tape to recover fibers from fabrics or other objects. A two-inch piece of clear tape is carefully placed on top of the fibers to be recovered. The tape is then removed and immediately attached to a clean glass microscope slide. The slide is placed in a labeled plastic slide holder for transportation to the laboratory.

Once the evidence is safely in the laboratory, the forensic hair and fiber examiner uses microtechniques to examine it. You can use the same techniques.

Using a magnifying glass and tweezers, carefully tease a few fibers from a fabric sample or other source. Depending on your preference, use one of the following preparation techniques: dry mount, wet mount, or permanent mount.

Dry Mount

Dry mounts are useful for adhering small opaque objects to paper slides so that they can be viewed under low-power magnification.

You will need a paper punch, a white index card cut to 1 inch x 3 inches, clear tape, and specimen material. Use Figure 24 as a guide. Use the paper punch to punch a hole in the center of the white index card. Lay the paper on a clean, smooth surface. Affix a piece of clear tape so that it covers the hole. Carefully peel the paper away from the smooth surface. Turn the paper over and sprinkle the dry objects intended for examination onto the transparent surface. Position the paper slide on the stage so that light will shine through the tape. Use the low-power scanning (4X) objective to begin your examination.

Wet Mount

Wet mounts are useful for observing small objects that can be suspended in a drop of water or are liquids themselves.

You will need a pipette or eyedropper, a sample, a glass microscope slide, tweezers, and a coverslip. Use Figure 25 as a guide. Using the pipette or eyedropper, place a drop containing the sample on a clean glass slide. Carefully, using the tweezers,

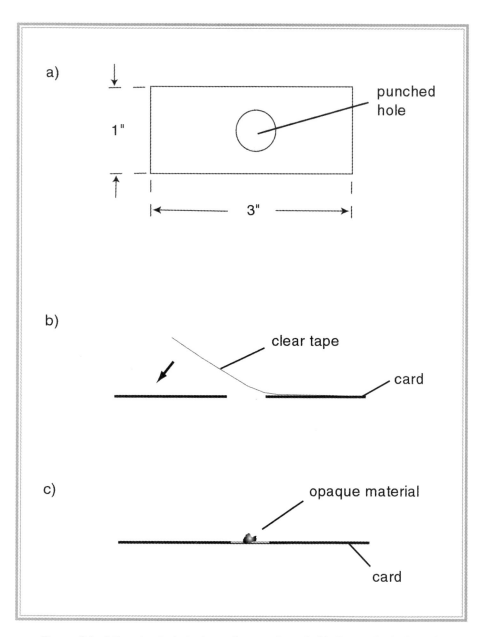

a)

1"

3"

punched
hole

b)

clear tape

card

c)

opaque material

card

Figure 24. a) Punch a hole in 1 in x 3 in card stock. b) Cover the hole with a piece of clear tape. c) Sprinkle trace evidence on sticky tape surface. Position the hole on the stage so that light can penetrate. Observe using a compound microscope at 40X.

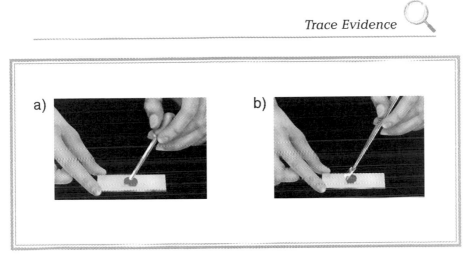

Figure 25. a) Add a drop containing the sample to be examined to a clean microscope slide. b) Use tweezers to add a coverslip.

lower the coverslip over the drop so that the drop spreads evenly without creating air bubbles.

Permanent Mount

Permanent mounts are useful for making long-lasting preparations of dry objects.

You will need a paper clip, medicine dropper, corn syrup, glass microscope slide, tweezers, a dry specimen, paper toweling, and a coverslip.

Uncoil the paper clip to form a paper clip probe, as shown in Figure 26. Use the medicine dropper to deposit a drop of corn syrup (mounting medium) the size of a pea in the center of the clean glass microscope slide. Use tweezers to place the dry specimen on the drop of mounting medium. Position the specimen with the paper clip probe. Use paper toweling to wipe the probe clean if it picks up any mounting medium. Carefully lay the coverslip down directly onto the drop. Gently spread the drop outward by applying gentle pressure to the center of the coverslip using the paper clip probe.

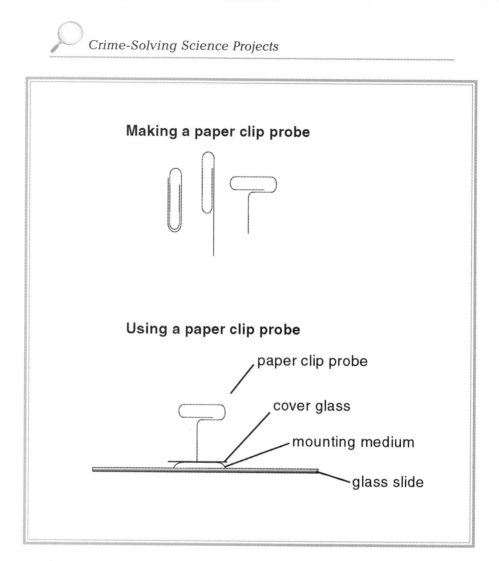

Making a paper clip probe

Using a paper clip probe

paper clip probe

cover glass

mounting medium

glass slide

Figure 26. Apply slight pressure using a paper clip probe to evenly spread out the mounting medium.

You can look at the fibers first with a magnifying glass. Then, place the slide on the microscope stage and examine individual fibers first under low (40–50X) magnification under even lighting. Switch to a higher magnification. Make notes and drawings of your observations in your notebook. Use the following checklist and the section "Natural and Synthetic Fibers" on pages 95–97 to organize your laboratory work.

Fiber Examination Checklist

- Fiber type (animal, plant, synthetic)
- Fiber description (microstructure, thickness, length, twist, color, etc.)
- If animal, determine source (compare to "Natural and Synthetic Fibers" section)
- If human, determine whether it is vellus, terminal, pulled, pigmented, curly, etc.
- If plant, determine source (compare to "Natural and Synthetic Fibers" section)
- If synthetic, determine composition (polyester, nylon, rayon)
- Note any unusual appearance, damage, etc.

Always record notes and analysis results in your laboratory notebook. Careful and complete information is all-important to practicing forensic science. If possible, use a camera attached to the microscope to make a photographic record of your microscopic observations. See Appendix A for photomicrography tips.

Science Projects You Can Do

Make a "reference standards collection" for hairs.

Collect hair types from a variety of sources and store them in sealed coin envelopes. Visit both a beautician and a barber and ask for hair samples. Your collection should include the following types: scalp hairs from Caucasian, Asian, and African-American people; curly hair; graying hair; bleached and dyed hair. Also try to obtain samples of vellus, eyelash, and facial hairs.

Collect animal hair types. A good place to begin is by visiting a pet grooming shop and asking permission to collect cat and dog hairs. Expand your collection by including hamster, guinea pig, and gerbil hair types. If possible, visit a taxidermist and ask if you can have samples of other animal hairs.

Use Figure 26 as a guide in making permanent mounts of your collected samples. Mount complete hairs lengthwise on the microscope slide. You might need to purchase rectangular coverslips from a science supply house. Label the slides. These finished slides will serve as comparison standards for your investigations.

Create a poster that explains how you assembled your reference standards collection. If possible, use drawings or photomicrographs to illustrate hair types.

Is melanin the only pigment in human hair?

Melanin is a brown-black pigment. Does the distribution of this pigment within the cortex account for all possible natural hair coloring? Examine terminal hairs from at least 10 individuals having the following natural (untreated) hair coloring: black, red, brown, yellow blond, white blond. Make your observations under a microscope at 100X. Create a data table that illustrates your findings. Use colored pencils to accurately represent what you observe under the microscope.

Refer to Figure 21 and take note of the presence of air spaces (cortical fusi), which contribute to light-colored hair. Does your observational data point to any connection between the number of air spaces and hair lightness?

Predict the relative age of humans.

Melanin production is gradually reduced as we age. Can this aging process be predicted? Obtain hair samples from individuals of various ages with similar natural hair color. Make a hair time line by placing hair strands next to each other in ascending age order. Make either a clear tape or permanent mount preparation. Create an illustrated record of your observations in your notebook using colored pencils to accurately represent hair coloration.

Demonstrate Locard's principle.

Conduct an experiment that demonstrates that every contact leaves a trace. Wash a T-shirt to remove any attached stray fibers. Dry alone in a clothes dryer. Put on the shirt and conduct various contact exercises: rolling on a carpet, roughhousing with a friend, playing with the family dog, wearing a sweater. Keep an exact log of each activity in your notebook. How many various fiber types can you recover? Can you match the fibers collected by the shirt to other, similar fibers at each recorded scene?

Once you are proficient at collecting fiber evidence at home, ask a friend to conduct the same exercise at his or her house. See if you can forensically trace your friend's journey. How good are you at trace evidence recovery?

Assess your forensic fiber analyzing skills.

Carefully clean the lint screen of your family's clothes dryer. Dry various types of known fabrics. Record these in your laboratory notebook. Collect the lint from the lint screen. Can you demonstrate complete fiber type recovery? Carefully separate fibers from collected lint and compare against fibers removed from the dried clothing. Be sure to include as many fabric fiber types as possible.

Casebook: Case of the Medullary Core

A brutal crime has been committed. A young man with blond hair has been killed by an act of violence. The crime scene investigators have recovered hair fiber evidence at the scene. A number of eyewitnesses have identified an individual of Asian decent observed near the area where the body was found at about the time of the slaying. Figure 27 shows photomicrographs of hairs found on the body that do not belong to the victim. You have been called in to conduct an expert analysis of this evidence and to advise the district attorney and police if there is enough physical evidence to consider the Asian individual a suspect.

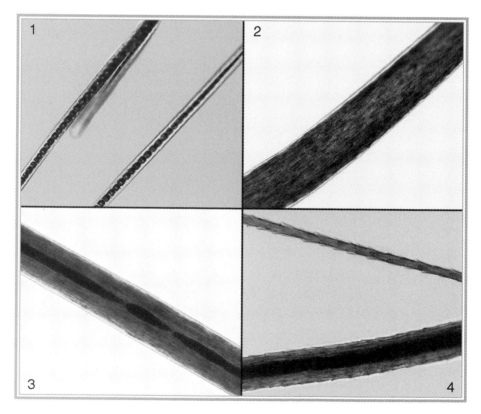

Figure 27. Hair fibers recovered from victim.

Appendix A:

Forensic Techniques

Using a Camera to Record Information

A camera is an important forensic documentation tool. Your choice of camera should reflect your intended use. Disposable 35-mm cameras are fine for recording general mock crime scene information. However, you will need a single lens reflex (SLR) camera for close-up imaging of documents and other similar materials.

Special adapters, compatible with your SLR camera, can be fitted to the eyepiece of a compound microscope for microscopic imaging. You will have to visit a local photography dealer who supports your camera type. The dealer will have catalogs that list the necessary adapters. Science supply companies also carry inexpensive instant photography cameras that mount over almost any compound or stereomicroscope eyepiece. See "Photography Tips" in this appendix for how to use an inexpensive fixed-focus camera to photograph microscopic images.

Imaging Things Close Up

Macrophotography is an important forensic tool. Photographing fibers, trace evidence, and documents requires close-up or "macro" photographic techniques. Macrophotography is a special branch of technical photography that begins where the closest focus of a standard lens leaves off—about one-tenth the actual size imaged by a standard 50-mm focal lens for everyday picture taking.

Close-up imaging techniques center on extending the camera lens using either mechanical or optical extension methods. As you extend the lens away from the film plane, the image-to-object ratio increases. For example, a standard 50-mm SLR lens must be extended 50 mm beyond its normal position, where the image-to-object ratio is 1:10, to obtain an image-to-object ratio of 1:1 at the film plane. The subject appears on film at its actual size.

Extension Tubes

Extension tubes incrementally extend the camera lens away from the film plane to position a larger image on the film. They can be metal rings or tubes used singly or in groups. These mechanical extension devices are available at camera stores or through photographic mail order companies. Tubes can be found in lengths from 5 mm up to 150 mm. They are usually supplied in sets of three, and a common grouping is for 6, 18, and 25 mm.

Close-up Lenses

Using an optical extension system attached to the front of your 35-mm camera lens, the camera can approach closer to the subject than the normal close focus its own lens would allow. Use Table A-1 as a guide to using close-up lenses.

TABLE A-1. CLOSE-UP LENS CHART

Close-up Lens	Lens-to-Subject Distance	Approximate Field Size (using a 50-mm lens)
+1	1000 mm	18 x 27 in
+2	500 mm	9 x 13.5 in
+3	333 mm	6 x 9 in
+4	250 mm	4.5 x 6.75 in
+5	200 mm	3.6 x 5.1 in
+6	167 mm	3 x 4.5 in

Copy Stands and Hard Stands

To achieve crisp, clear images, it is necessary to keep the camera from moving during long exposure times common in macrophotography. Use a tripod, copy stand, or Discovery Scope hard stand.

A copy stand allows for stabilizing the camera and lighting a subject. It is most useful in photographing rather flat subjects such as documents or photographic images. Use a tungsten flood as the light source; light from the side. Commercial stands are available or you can rig you own.

A hard stand is an inflexible attachment support that physically links the camera and the subject so that there is no chance of vibration spoiling the shot. An excellent choice is the Discovery Scope camera adapter for use with both 35-mm cameras and video cameras.

Photography Tips

You can use an inexpensive fixed focused digital camera or a conventional camera having a fixed-focus (integral) lens to capture microscopic images. These cameras have a single, fixed focus (usually at infinity). Using Figure 28 as a guide, position the front surface of the camera's lens at or very near the eyepoint. Devise a method to hold the camera in place over the microscope eyepiece. One method is to cut a piece of black PVC tubing of the correct diameter and length so that when it is placed atop the head of the microscope, and when the camera lens is inserted into its other opening, the correct eyepoint distance is maintained. This allows quick access for eyepiece viewing and assures that the camera can be placed back into the same position. Use fast (high ASA/ISO) film and allow for a very bright image to obtain a useful exposure.

One simple way to photograph portions of documents is to attach them to a white card held in a Discovery Scope hard stand (see Figure 29). Use available outdoor lighting along with extension tubes or close-up lenses with a 50-mm SLR lens to frame an enlarged image.

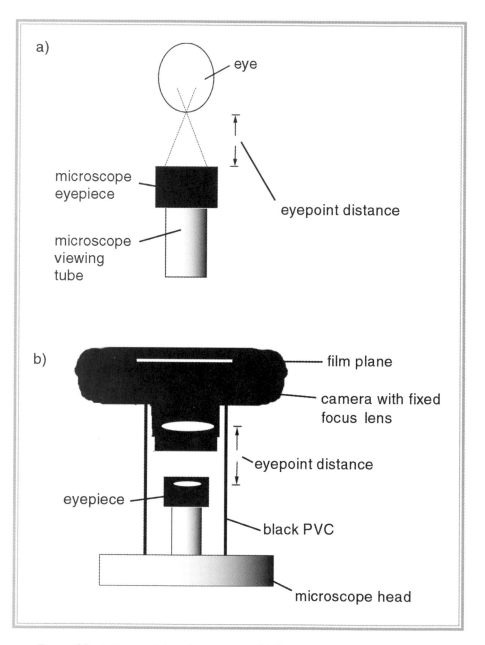

a)

eye

microscope
eyepiece

eyepoint distance

microscope
viewing
tube

b)

film plane

camera with fixed
focus lens

eyepoint distance

eyepiece

black PVC

microscope head

Figure 28. a) Determining the eyepoint. b) Positioning the camera lens at the eyepoint. You can determine the position of the eyepoint by holding a piece of white paper on top of the eyepiece, then slowly raising it. A bright circle will appear on the paper. This circle will become smaller then larger as the distance from the eyepiece increases. The position where the circle is smallest is the eyepoint.

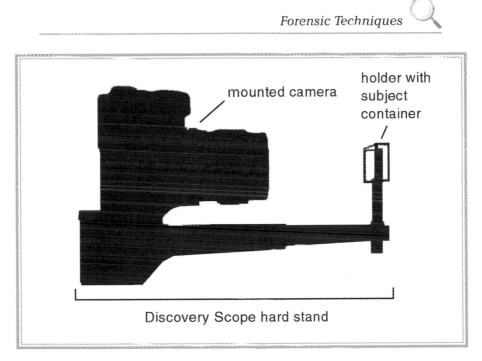

Figure 29. Using a Discovery Scope hard stand with a 35mm SLR camera. The camera base is screwed into the hard stand base. An extension tube holds a clear subject container to be photographed.

Using a Microscope

Always use indirect lighting when illuminating objects. Never use the microscope mirror to capture direct sunlight. Because the mirror concentrates light rays, you could permanently damage your eyes.

1. Begin by examining any object using the lowest-power objective. Place a glass slide on the stage with the center of the slide over the hole in the stage, specimen side up.

2. Adjust the light source (flat mirror surface or illuminator) and iris or disk diaphragm until light passes through the specimen. With the low-power objective in place, use the coarse adjustment knob to lower the objective until it is about ¾ inch (1.9 cm) from the surface of the coverslip.

3. Look through the eyepiece and slowly raise the objective with the coarse adjustment knob until the specimen is in approximate focus. Then use the fine adjustment knob to bring the

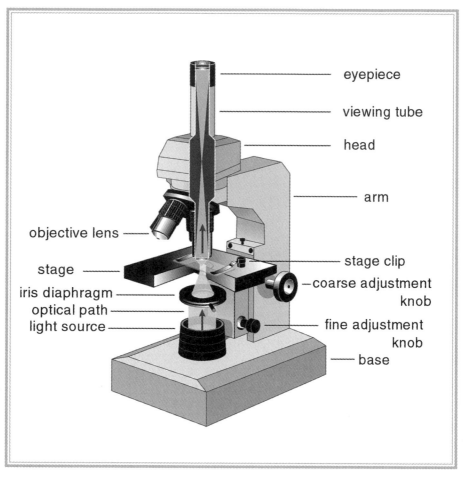

Figure 30. Compound microscope parts

image into sharp focus. Change the focus often, using fine focus to view all parts of your specimen.

4. Adjust the disk or iris diaphragm for best lighting. You will need more light (a wider diaphragm opening) at higher magnifications.

5. When rotating higher-power objectives into the optical path, you will feel a click as the objective locks into place. To avoid jamming the objective lens into the slide preparation, sharpen the focus using the fine adjustment knob only. Never focus under high power with the coarse adjustment knob.

6. Never touch lenses.

7. Keep the microscope stage clean and dry. If any liquids are spilled, wipe them up immediately with paper towels.

8. Resolution = Information: What you see with increased magnification depends upon the resolution of your scope. Optical resolution is determined by how well the viewing eye can distinguish the individual parts of an object. Most microscope objectives are labeled 4X, 10X, and 40X. Resolution is greatest at 40X, while size and depth of field (the zone that is in focus) are greatest at 4X.

9. To determine how greatly magnified the field of view is, multiply the number inscribed on the eyepiece lens by the number on the objective being used. For example:

   eyepiece (5X) x objective (4X) = total magnification (20X).

10. To estimate the size of your field of view, secure a 1-inch-square piece of 1-mm-ruled graph paper to a glass microscope slide and center it in the field of view. Make sure that one edge just touches the outer rim of the field. Since the distance between ruled lines is 1 mm (1000 µm), the size of the field for your microscope can be estimated.

    In general, the following field sizes are good estimates for a microscope having a 10X eyepiece:

objective		size of field
10X	low-power objective	1600 µm
43X	high dry objective	375 µm
100X	oil-immersion objective	160 µm

Appendix B:

Science Supply Companies

Materials Guide

Although most materials can be obtained through local sources, there are some specific materials required for certain projects. Your science teacher may allow you access to certain materials such as a microscope or electronic balance.

The following table tells you which companies carry the materials you will need. The supplier number corresponds to the numbered list of companies on page 119.

Chapter 1. What Is Forensic Science, Anyway?

Materials	Suppliers
Science Fair Project Materials	3, 4, 5, 6, 7
Forensic Science Kits	3, 4, 5, 6, 7

Chapter 3. Fingerprints

Materials	Suppliers
Inkless Fingerprinting Materials	7

Chapter 7. Trace Evidence

Materials	Suppliers
Fiber and Hair Set	1

Appendix A: Forensic Techniques

Materials	Suppliers
Discovery Scope Hard Stand	2
Discovery Scope Handheld Microscope	2
Microscope Cameras and Adapters	3, 4, 5, 6
Microscopy Audiovisual Materials	2

To order from a science supply company, ask your science teacher if you may borrow a catalog from the company so that you can assemble information about order numbers and prices. You should try to coordinate your order through a science teacher who might also need supplies. Most companies accept orders through the mail, over the phone, via fax, or through a Web site. Have a check, money order, or credit card number ready when you place your order.

1 Arbidar Company
26 M Street South
Sula, Montana 59871-9703
Phone: (406) 821-3426
FAX: (406) 821-3426
e-mail: arbidar@montana.com

2 BioMEDIA Associates
P.O. Box 457
Loomis, CA 95650
Phone: (916) 663-3304

3 Carolina Biological Supply Company
2700 York Road
Burlington, NC 27215
Phone: (800) 334-5551
FAX: (800) 222-7112
e-mail: cbass@carolina.com
Web site: www.carolina.com

4 Fisher Scientific Company
Fisher Science Education Division
485 South Frontage Road
Burr Ridge, IL 60521
Phone: (800) 955-1177
FAX: (800) 955-0740
e-mail: info@fisheredu.com
Web site: www.fisheredu.com

5 Flinn Scientific, Inc.
P.O. Box 219
Batavia, IL 60510
Phone: (800) 452-1261
FAX: (630) 879-6962
e-mail: flinn@flinnsci.com
Web site: www.flinnsci.com

6 Frey Scientific
100 Paragon Parkway
Mansfield, OH 44903
Phone: (800) 225-3739
FAX: (877) 256-3739

7 Neo/Sci Corporation
P.O. Box 22729
Rochester, NY 14692-2729
Phone: (800) 526-6689
FAX: (800) 657-7523
e-mail: jconiber@neosci.com
Web site: www.neosci.com

Appendix C:

Casebook Solutions

Chapter 2 "Case of the Runaway Hot Rod"

Your analysis of all three paint chip fragments shows that they are not alike. Paint fragment "A," recovered from a crumpled area of the hood of the suspect's vehicle matches paint fragment "C" recovered from the victim's outer clothing. Paint fragment "B" also recovered from the victim's clothing, does not match, but appears to be automobile paint. Further analysis is necessary. You advise the police that additional samples should be taken from the impact area of the suspect's vehicle. Your preliminary report states that a definite association between the victim and the suspect's vehicle can be made.

Chapter 3 "Case of the Digital Image"

As an experienced forensic investigator, you compare both right thumbprints by analyzing eight to twelve additional ridgeline details. You also compare prints for areas of obvious mismatching. Your analysis is shown below. It conclusively points out the following:

- The width of some ridgelines were changed, as were many ridgeline details—but not enough.

- Ten matching ridgeline areas still proved an identical match.

Kaprikosh was not as skilled as he had thought. An investigation by the local police department has begun.

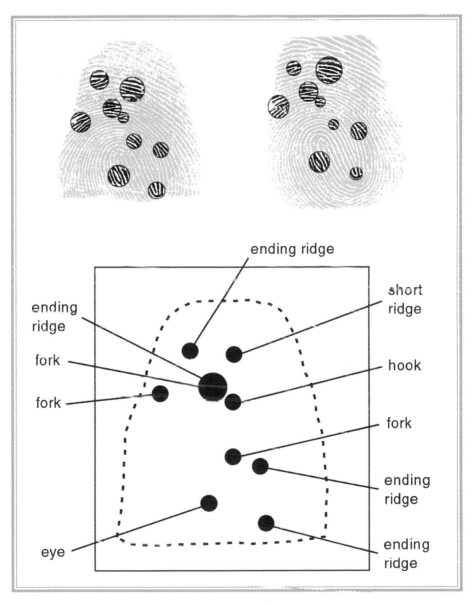

Figure 31. Case of the Digital Image.

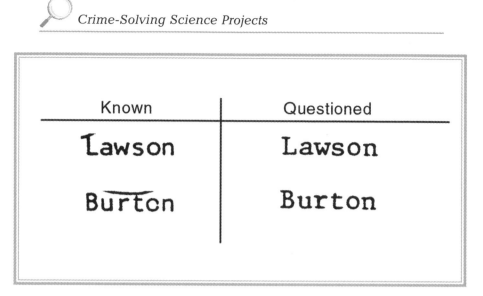

Known	Questioned
Lawson	**Lawson**
Burton	**Burton**

Figure 32. Case of the Altered Photocopy. The known type is from the closing signature and the questioned type is from the body of the letter. (See the original letter on page 68).

Chapter 4 "Case of the Altered Photocopy"

Lawson Burton's signature is genuine. However, the document is not a continuous typescript. Figure 32 shows the analysis:

- The typescript, beginning with the complimentary close, is from a different—but closely matching—font than the body of the document. Note the different letter style in both *Lawson* and *Burton*.

- The signature had come from another document that used a different, and unique, font style. Miss Carpenter used a closely matching font for the body of the letter.

- Notice that there are evident paste lines to the right of the signature.

Also, there were no minutes kept at the trial of Major André. A record of the trial exists on folio sheets, as attested to by numerous historical witnesses.

Chapter 5 "Case of the Rare Autographs"

Your standard analysis conclusively proves that the Clinton signature is an autopen pattern and not a rare presidential signature. The jagged lines and even weight of the ink are telltale signs. The autograph by Mickey Mantle is authentic.

By making a photocopy of each signature on a clear acetate sheet, putting together the known and questioned ones, and holding them up to the light together for comparison, you find that the Clinton signatures are an identical match but that the Mantle signatures are not. You also determine that the line in the Clinton signatures is a little shaky and its width is equal and does not vary. Knowing that no two authentic signatures are identical, you advise your client that the Clinton signature is an autopen. The Mantle signatures, although close in resemblance, are not identical and have a varied line width; they are authentic.

Chapter 6 "Case of the Bloodstained Pavement"

Based upon the shape of the bloodstains, they are not castoffs. The bloodstains are consistent with those of drops falling at a 90-degree angle at a height of 3 and 4 feet—the approximate distance between the ground and a hand hanging from the side or being held at waist level in an upright adult. The suspect is cleared.

Chapter 7 "Case of the Medullary Core"

The physical evidence does not place an individual of Asian decent at the crime scene. Both animal and human hairs were recovered and photographed. Samples 1 and 4 are of cat hair. Their medullary indexes are greater than 0.5. They also show distinct spinous type cuticular scales, typical in cat hair. The remaining samples are of human hair. Both Samples 2 and 3 have a medullary index of between 0 and 0.33. In these hairs, the medullary core is either interrupted (Sample 3) or absent (Sample 2). No human hair samples were recovered that had a continuous medullary core, as would be found in a person of Asian descent. Your report should tell the authorities that this individual should not be considered a suspect and that they should continue the search for an individual whose hair either has an interrupted medullary core or is without a medullary core.

Further Reading

Ahouse, Jeremy, and C. Babcock. *Fingerprinting*. Berkeley, Calif.: University of California, Lawrence Hall of Science, 1998.

Bowers, Vivien. *Crime Science: How Investigators Use Science to Track Down the Bad Guys*. Toronto: Owl Books, 1997.

Foltz-Jones, Charlotte. *Fingerprints & Talking Bones: How Real-Life Crimes Are Solved*. New York: Delacorte Press, 1997.

Gardner, Robert. *Crime Lab 101: Experimenting with Crime Detection*. New York: Walker & Co., 1994.

Grave, Eric. *Using the Microscope: A Guide for Naturalists*. New York: Dover Publications, Inc., 1991.

Houde, John. *Crime Lab: A Guide for Nonscientists*. Ventura, Calif.: Calico Press, 1999.

Levine, Shar. *Fun with Your Microscope*. New York: Sterling Publishing Co., Inc., 1999.

Rainis, Kenneth G. *Exploring with a Magnifying Glass*. New York: Franklin Watts, Inc., 1991.

Wiese, James. *Detective Science: 40 Crime-Solving, Case-Breaking, Crook-Catching Activities for Kids*. New York: John Wiley & Sons, Inc., 1996.

Internet Addresses

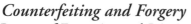

Counterfeiting and Forgery
Bureau of Engraving and Printing.
    <http://www.moneyfactory.com>

Crime Laboratories
California Criminalistics Institute. July 26, 1999.
    <http://www.ns.net/cci>

Federal Bureau of Investigation.
    <http://www.fbi.gov/homepage.htm>

Kern County District Attorney. *Forensic Science
Crime Lab.* "Virtual Tours."
    <http://www.co.kern.ca.us/DA/science/Virtual.htm>

United States Postal Inspection Service.
    "Postal Inspection Service Crime Lab."
    <http://www.usps.gov/websites/depart/inspect/crimelab.htm>

Crime Scene Photography
University of California. *Crime Scene Investigator.* "Crime
Scene and Evidence Photography." February 29, 2000.
    <http://police2.ucr.edu/photo.html>

Forensic Science Careers
Forensic DNA Consulting. *Education in Forensic Science.* "Careers in
Forensic Science." © 1998–2000.
    <http://www.forensicdna.com/careers.htm>

Microscopy
Thomas E. Jones. *History of the Light Microscope.* © 1997.
    <http://www.utmem.edu/personal/thjones/hist/hist_mic.htm>

Paint Analysis
Welsh Color and Conservation, Inc. "Analysis of Historic Paints and
Wallpapers." <http://www.welshcolor.com/sampling.html>

Index